TRY-ITS
FOR BROWNIE GIRL SCOUTS

Girl Scouts of the USA
420 Fifth Avenue
New York, N.Y. 10018-2798

National President
Connie L. Matsui

National Executive Director
Marsha Johnson Evans

National Director, Membership and Program
Sharon Woods Hussey

Director, Program Development
Harriet S. Mosatche, Ph.D.

Project Directors
Rosemarie Cryan
Harriet S. Mosatche, Ph.D.

Authors
Melissa Algranati, Chris Bergerson, María Cabán, Rosemarie Cryan, Dee Ebersole, Toni Eubanks, Lauraine
Merlini, Harriet S. Mosatche, Ph.D., Patricia Paddock

Director, Publishing
Suzanna Penn

Senior Editor
David Sahatdjian

Manager, Creative Design and Production
Christina Cannard-Seward

Design and Production
Kaeser and Wilson Design Ltd.

Illustrators
Eveline Feldman Allred, pp. 61, 107; Kelly Bender, pp. 21 (left), 23, 27, 41, 46 (right), 58, 72, 74, 114, 115 (lower
right; Len Epstein, pp. 35, 43; Richard Goldberg, pp. 10, 19, 45, 70, 71, 118, 120, 121, 134, 136, 137, 161; Lisa
Marchitello, cover, pp. 6, 16, 56, 84, 144; DJ Simison, pp. 28, 29, 38, 40, 46 (left), 51, 95, 96, 97, 120, 128, 143,
148; Rosiland Solomon, pp. 91, 92, 93, 110, 111, 116, 127, 130, 131, 139, 164, 165; Liz Wheaton, pp. 9, 15, 18,
20, 21 (right), 47, 62, 63, 65, 69, 73, 78, 89, 101, 104, 115, 135, 166

Photographers
Lori Adamski-Peek, pp. 5, 31, 32; Peter Brandt, cover, p. 98; Corbis, p. 11

Inquiries related to *Try-Its for Brownie Girl Scouts* should be directed to Membership and Program, Girl Scouts of the USA,
420 Fifth Avenue, New York, N.Y. 10018-2798.

© 2000 by Girl Scouts of the United States of America
All rights reserved
First Impression 2000
Printed in the United States of America
ISBN 13: 978-0-88441-605-0
ISBN 0-88441-605-4

20 19

Contents

My Try-It Record Keeper

Name of Try-It	Numbers of Completed Activities	Date Whole Try-It Finished
1.		
2.		
3.		
4.		
5.		
6.		
7.		
8.		
9.		
10.		
11.		
12.		
13.		
14.		
15.		

Introduction

TRY-IT MEANS JUST THAT. JUMP RIGHT IN. Get your hands dirty and your heart racing. Use your imagination. Learn a new hobby. Show everyone how good you are at an old one.

This book is just for you. You don't have to do the same Try-Its as your friends or your Girl Scout troop—unless, of course, you want to. **To earn a Try-It, complete four of the activities listed for that topic.** You and the other girls can then plan a Court of Awards ceremony as a special way to receive your Try-Its. Some troops or groups plan one Court of Awards at the end of the year. Others like to have these ceremonies more often. That's a decision you and the other girls in your troop or group can make with your leader.

Looking for things to do?

Check out the online awards, like the Brownie Girl Scout Challenge Award at http://www.gogirlsonly.org/spotlight/.

The main thing is to have fun. Experiment! Explore! Learn! That's what Try-Its and Girl Scouting are all about.

1

Brownie Girl Scouts, Let's Get Started!

Brownie Girl Scouts
Around the World

From Argentina to Zimbabwe, Girl Scouts and Girl Guides are having fun, helping others, learning new things, and pitching in to help their communities.

1. What Do They Call...?

Girls your age are called Brownie Girl Scouts in the U.S. But what are they called in other countries? Match each term with the correct country. How do you know if you have the countries in the right order? When you circle the first letter of each country, you'll spell out a word that fits in the sentence below:

Country	Name	Write the Name of the Matching Country
Thailand	Minor Guides	....
Norway	Little Wings	....
Ghana	Zahras	....
Italy	Brownie Guides	....
Chile	Bluebirds	....
United Kingdom	Wolf Cubs	....
Sweden	Brownies	....
Oman	Ananse Guides	....

Girl _____ is fun!

2. Where in the World...?

Look at a map of the world. Choose three of these countries listed in Activity #1, and find out two facts about each of them.

3. Around the World

Learn a song, dance, or story from another country. Share what you learned with your Girl Scout troop or group, or with your family.

4. Create a Picture Book

Create a picture book of activities that your troop or group really likes to do. Draw pictures or use photos to illustrate the activities. Display your book during Girl Scout Week.

5. Global Games

Pick one of the games below and try it with your friends, family, or Girl Scout troop or group:

Music Mystery (Canada)

1. Divide the group into two teams. Team #1 is the band. Team #2 is the audience. Team #1 picks a song and beats out the rhythm of the song using pot lids, bells or other items.

2. Team #2 tries to guess the song and then sings along.

3. The teams switch roles. Team #2 becomes the band.

Jump Rope (China)

1. Create an elastic band of about 12 to 15 feet. You can buy this type of jump rope in toy stores.

2. Two girls place their feet on the inside of the band, standing far enough apart that the jump rope is tight.

3. A third girl is the jumper. She can jump over one rope and back over the same one. Or she can jump over one rope and then over the next rope.

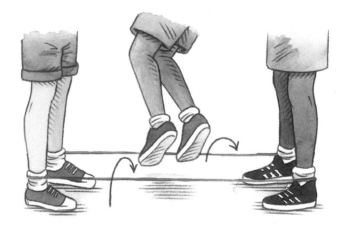

Brownie Girl Scouts Through the Years

Brownie Girl Scouting got started in the late 1920s. Many of the appliances we take for granted today had not yet been invented. Few people flew in airplanes, or used a phone to call long distance. Many of the other medicines people use today had not been discovered.

Choose from the following activities to learn more about the past.

Try It!

1. Meals

Travel back in time with your Girl Scout troop or group. Choose a decade (1920s, 1930s, 1940s, 1950s, 1960s) and create a snack that Brownie Girl Scouts would have eaten then. If your period is the 1920s, you don't want to serve frozen foods, since they weren't available until many years later. And don't use plastic cups or plates. Plastic dining materials weren't in common use until the 1950s.

2. Clothes

Pick a time period and create outfits that would have been in fashion then. As you wear your outfits, try to imagine being in those same clothes years ago. How should you move and sit in them? How is your outfit different from the clothes you wear today?

Find out what girls' hairstyles were like back in the decade you've chosen. Wear your hair in that same fashion.

1960's

1950's

1940's

1920's

3. Entertainment

Up until the 1940s no one had television sets. Even in the early 1950s not too many people had them. People played card games and word games, told jokes, and listened to the radio together. But movies have been a popular form of entertainment since the silent films in the early part of the 1900s. Pick a time period (1920s, 1930s, 1940s, 1950s, 1960s), and choose songs to play and movies to watch from those years. (For example, *Snow White* was playing in theaters in the 1930s.) With your friends, learn a card game that people were playing back then. Or find a game that your parents or grandparents remember playing.

4. Sing a Song

Travel back in time. Choose a decade (1920s, 1930s, 1940s, 1950s, 1960s, 1970s, 1980s) and learn a song that was popular then. Sing it for your troop or group, or your family. Then teach it to them.

5. Language of the Times

Ask people of different ages about expressions they used as children. Look at movies, TV shows, or magazines from those years. How did girls your age talk? What were the "cool" words or sayings? How did girls your age act? What were other manners of the time you've picked?

6. Service to Others

Pick a time period, and plan and carry out a service project Girl Scouts would have done back then. Did you choose the 1920s? Girls packed and dedicated holiday baskets for the Salvation Army. In the 1940s, they rolled bandages for the American men and women serving in World War II. They also ran paper and aluminum drives. In the 1980s, girls your age contributed to food drives for local food pantries. Today, a service project might involve recycling paper or cans or collecting children's videos to donate to a local hospital.

Cookies Count

Every year, Girl Scouts across the country sell Girl Scout Cookies as a fun way to support their projects and activities. It's a great way to learn new things—how to get along with people, work with a team, set goals, and improve your math skills. Girl Scout Cookies taste good and lots of people buy them. Your leader will help you with the cookie sale, and remember:

1. You must have permission from a parent or guardian.

2. Your parent or guardian must always know where you are when you are helping with the cookie sale.

3. You must always have an adult with you when you sell Girl Scout Cookies.

4. You must not sell Girl Scout Cookies over the Internet, but you may e-mail friends and family to let them know about the sale.

1. Setting Goals

Did you ever wish you could win a prize for being the best at something? Or buy someone a special birthday present? Or get an "A" in school? Most of the time, there are ways to reach your goal. Making plans is important.

With your Girl Scout friends, set some goals for things you would like to do. It could be having a holiday party, going on a picnic, having enough money to go on a special trip, or having money for a service project.

With the help of your leader, think of the things your troop or group would like to do and make some plans.

• How much would it cost?

• How would you get there?

• Who would help?

• How will the cookie sale help you reach your goals?

Try It!

2. Good Manners

Good manners, including being polite and always saying "please" and "thank you," are an important part of selling Girl Scout Cookies. Decide how you and your friends can practice good manners. You might even write thank-you notes from the whole troop.

Dear Mr. Smith:
    Thank you for buying 10 boxes of Girl Scout Cookies for your son's party. We are saving for a trip to the 4-H farm. The money will help a lot.

Sincerely,
The Brownie Girl Scouts
from Troop 404

3. Being a Good Friend or Neighbor

Girl Scouts try to be helpful and kind to their friends and neighbors. Think about ways to help others through the cookie sale. For example, set aside some of the troop money to buy boxes of cookies and give them to someone as a present, perhaps a child who is sick or a senior citizen who is celebrating a birthday. This may also be an opportunity to spend time with someone who would enjoy some company.

4. Fun with Change

If you are going to buy or sell something, you need to know how to make change. Find out how much a box of Girl Scout Cookies costs. Ask your leader or another adult to help you learn about counting money. How many pennies are in a dollar? How many nickels and dimes? How many quarters? Practice buying and selling cookies and making change.

5. Fun on the Job

There are lots of jobs connected with buying and selling cookies and other products. Find out about some of them by taking a little trip around the neighborhood with your leader or another adult. Stop by a bakery to see how cookies are made. Go to a supermarket to find out how products are displayed. Visit a store and ask a salesperson to explain her job.

6. Cookie Talk

Practice what you would say to a customer (the person who is doing the buying). What would you say about the cookies? Do you know what they taste like and how much they cost? Be able to tell the customer what your troop or group plans to do with the money earned from the boxes of cookies that are sold and some of the other special things Girl Scouts do.

Girl Scout Ways

Being a Girl Scout makes you part of a very special group of people! Here are some activities that show some of the things Girl Scouts everywhere know.

1. The Girl Scout Law

Create a puppet show, coloring book, poem, or play that tells about two parts of the Girl Scout Law. Show it to other Girl Scouts or to girls who want to become Girl Scouts.

2. Special Girl Scout Ways

Read the section "What Makes Brownie Girl Scouting Special?" in the *Brownie Girl Scout Handbook*. Practice the hand signs and traditions listed below and show them to someone who is new to Girl Scouting:

• Girl Scout handshake.
• Girl Scout sign.
• Quiet sign.
• Friendship circle.
• Friendship squeeze.

3. S'mores

A S'more is a special sweet treat that Girl Scouts love to make. You might want to try it on a camping trip or at a cookout. Do you know why they're called *S'mores*?

You will need:
• Graham crackers.
• Large marshmallows.
• Milk chocolate bars.
• A long stick or roasting wire to hold over the fire.

1. Break a chocolate bar so that it is the same size as the graham cracker or smaller. Put the chocolate on top of the graham cracker.

2. Put one or two marshmallows on the end of the stick.

3. Use the stick to hold the marshmallows over the fire, but not too close.

4. When the marshmallows start to melt just a little, take them off the stick and put them on top of the chocolate bar square.

5. Put another graham cracker on top of the marshmallows.

6. Eat it! And you will want s'more.

Note: Whenever you are using fire in the outdoors, in a fireplace, or anywhere else, you must have an adult helping you.

4. Sit–Upon

Girl Scouts make sit-upons to use when the ground is damp or too hot or cold, or they want to keep their clothes clean. You can make your own to use at troop meetings, camping events, or other Girl Scout get-togethers. Follow these steps and look at the pictures for help.

You will need:
• A large piece of waterproof material (like an old plastic tablecloth, shower curtain, or plastic garbage bag).
• Newspapers or other stuffing.
• A yarn needle.
• Yarn or string.

1. Cut the waterproof material into two large squares big enough for you to sit on.

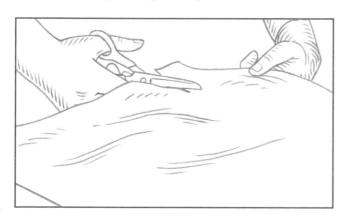

2. Put newspapers or old rags between the two squares to form a cushion.

3. Sew the two squares together with yarn or string, using the yarn needle. Have an adult show you how to use the needle

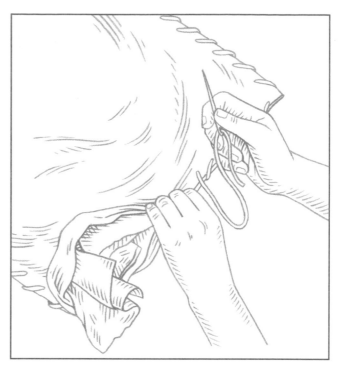

safely. Be sure to sew completely around the edges of the sit-upon.

5. Be Prepared

Girl Scouting's motto is: "Be Prepared!" Talk with other Girl Scouts about how you can help your troop or group, school, family, and friends prepare for two or three of the situations below:

• Bad weather.

• A house fire.

• The power going out.

• An injury like a cut or fall.

• A long trip.

What other situations should you and your family prepare for? You can get some ideas from Chapter 2, "Taking Care of Yourself," in the *Brownie Girl Scout Handbook*.

Taking Care of Yourself

Art to Wear

Art hangs on walls in museums and galleries, but that's not all. The ceramic mug you sip your hot chocolate from may also be an example of art.

Try the activities below and develop your own artistic abilities.

1. T-Shirt Art

Turn a plain T-shirt or sweatshirt into your own work of art.

You will need:
- A plain T-shirt or sweatshirt.
- Pencil.
- Cardboard.
- Clothespins or large paper clips.
- Fabric paint.

1. Place the cardboard inside the T-shirt or sweatshirt. Clip it in place with the clothespins or paper clips. This will make it easier to draw or paint your design.

2. Use your pencil to sketch a picture on the T-shirt or sweatshirt.

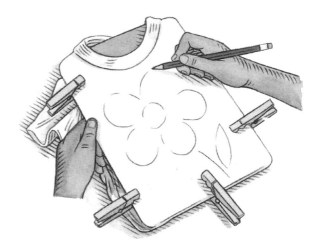

3. Use the fabric paint to add color to your drawing. You can simply paint over the outline or color it in.

If you prefer, you can create a design instead of a picture. For example, you can use lines and shapes in different colors to make an interesting pattern.

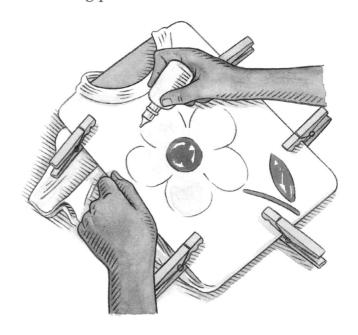

3. Face Paint

Have a face-painting party. Make certain an adult is present. Be sure to use makeup and paints that are made just for the face. You can find these in toy or crafts stores. If possible, invite a makeup artist to your troop to demonstrate different kinds of face painting.

2. Decorate Your Clothes

With heavy thread, sew small, colorful beads or buttons on the edges of your socks or around the neck of a T-shirt or sweatshirt. Use fabric paints to design your shoelaces with polka dots and stripes. You can decorate dolls' clothes or make a special collar for a pet.

19

4. Papier-Mâché

Papier-mâché is made from paper and glue. It's lots of fun to make and shape! Use the instructions that follow to make a papier-mâché bracelet.

You will need:
• A cardboard tube that fits loosely over your wrist.
• Scrap paper cut or torn into strips.
• Colored tissue paper, also cut or torn into strips.
• Scissors.
• A paste made of flour and water or liquid starch. (You can buy liquid starch in many crafts stores.)
• A shallow pan that can be thrown away.

1. Cut the cardboard tube to the width you want for your bracelet.

2. Tear or cut the scrap paper and the tissue paper into strips.

3. Make a paste in the pan by mixing flour and water. Use a cup of flour with 1 cup of water. Or, instead of flour and water, you can pour liquid starch into the pan and use it for paste.

4. Dip the scrap paper strips into your paste, and pull them out one at a time. Layer the strips. Use your fingers to mold and shape the strips. Don't worry about bumps.

5. For the last layers, use strips of colored tissue paper. Create patterns or a solid surface. Place the bracelet in a warm, dry place. The thicker your bracelet is, the longer it will take to dry. Liquid starch may take longer to dry than a paste made from flour and water.

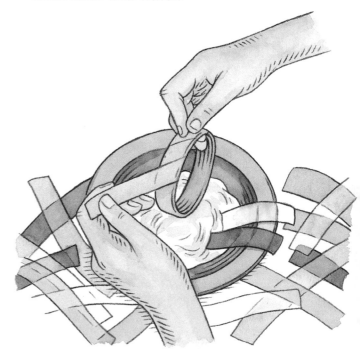

5. Mask Making

Many people around the world make masks for ceremonies, holidays, or dramatic events. Some masks are used to tell stories. Choose a holiday or special event and make a mask to celebrate it.

You will need:
- A paper bag.
- Bits of paper, yarn, or other materials.
- Crayons or paint.
- Glue.
- Scissors.

You can also use heavy cardboard as a base to make a mask that you hold to your face by a handle. (Chopsticks, Popsicle sticks, or pencils make good handles.)

Try It!

6. Knots

Use string, ribbon, rope, or cord to tie knots to make bracelets, necklaces, belts, and other things. This craft is called *macramé*. Look at the pictures for directions on how to make different kinds of knots. Using color can make your project more exciting.

Overhand Knot

Square Knot

Careers

Have you thought about what you would like to do when you grow up? This Try-It will help you explore some possibilities.

1. Autobiography

Make a list of all the things you like to do—it can include hobbies, schoolwork, sports, or anything at all. Discuss your list with an adult. Which of the things on your list are things people do on the job? Find out about a job that sounds like fun.

Soccer
baseball
tennis
Golf
Swimming
coloring
Reading
Gardening
playing with dogs.

2. Future Jobs

Many jobs that people have today did not even exist many years ago. Interview some adults to find out if they knew as children what jobs they wanted to have as adults. Think about how the world will be when you are older. Make a list of the new kinds of jobs you think will be available when you grow up that don't exist now.

Robot maintenance
Space tourism:
making flying cars

3. Women Pioneers

Find out about famous women inventors and explorers. What were some of the things they did? Can you find women who were pioneers in other fields? Share what you learn with your troop or group.

4. Career Charades

Divide the troop or group into two teams. Each team should take turns having a girl act out one of the jobs listed below. The other team has to guess what she is. Add other jobs to this list.

- Bank teller
- Computer programmer
- Bus driver
- Pharmacist
- Doctor
- Firefighter
- Veterinarian
- Musician
- TV reporter
- Astronaut
- Scientist
- Coach
- Electrician
- Teacher
- Chef
- Farmer
- Carpenter
- Book illustrator
- Photographer
- Web site designer

5. Learn to Earn

Learning how to handle money is important now and for when you get older. Read about money and budgets on pages 39-41 in the *Brownie Girl Scout Handbook*. With a group, plan one of the money-earning projects.

Try It!

6. It's Your Business

Many women own their own businesses. Create your own one-day business with other girls in your troop or group: for example, a jewelry store that will sell necklaces you've made or an art gallery that sells your one-of-a-kind paintings or clay sculptures.

Dancercize

Dancing is a great way to exercise. Tap your feet, kick your heels, and spin around while you combine dance and exercise.

1. Move to the Beat

Practice these movements to your favorite music:

1. March in place.

2. Step forward and backward and swing your arms to the sides.

3. Step sideways and swing your arms in circles.

4. Put your hands on your hips and move from side to side.

5. Walk in a circle, lifting your knees very high while clapping your hands.

Make up some of your own moves. Do them for at least 10-15 minutes.

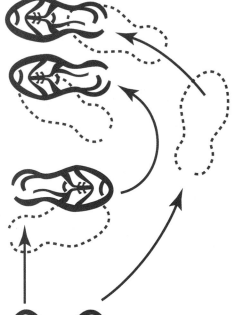

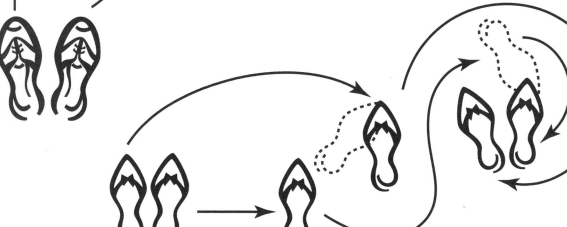

2. Dance on Stage

Watch a dance performance at a theater or community center, on an outdoor stage, or on television. What parts of the dance can you imitate?

3. My Own Dance

Make up a dance to your favorite song. Teach this dance to other girls.

4. Dance Party

Have a dance party with a group of friends.

You will need:
• Records, tapes, or CDs.
• A record player, CD player, tape player, or radio.
• Snacks.

1. Pick a time and place for a get-together with your friends.

2. Decide on the music. Each girl can bring her favorite dance music.

3. Teach each other dance steps.

4. Have a healthy snack for energy.

5. Follow the Leader

Take turns with other girls in being the leader in your troop. The leader should call out a movement and show everyone how to follow it. You can do these movements to start: climbing a ladder, reaching for the sun on tiptoes, moving like a windmill, touching toes with knees slightly bent. Think of others you can do.

6. A Dance Story

Use dance to tell a story. Use movement to express feelings such as fear, excitement, sadness, or surprise.

Eat Right, Stay Healthy

What you eat affects your health. Try these activities to learn more about good food.

1. The Foods We Eat

Food labels list ingredients starting with the largest amount down to the smallest amounts. They also show how much of each nutrient (such as minerals and vitamins) is in each food serving. Calcium, which helps your bones grow strong, is an example of a mineral. Vitamin C, found in orange juice, is an example of a vitamin.

Look at lists of ingredients from cereal cartons, cake-mix boxes, and canned and frozen foods. Many times, sugar or salt is added to food as a flavoring. Sugar is sometimes called corn syrup, sucrose, glucose, or fructose.

Compare three labels and decide which food is the best for you. When deciding what is a healthy food, check the food pyramid on page 48 in your handbook.

2. Smart Shopper

Help your family make up a grocery list. Write down foods that your family likes to eat during the week. Look at the list with the person who does the food shopping in your home. Go with her or him to the grocery store to help choose good foods. Then plan at least one meal using what you have learned from the food pyramid.

3. Dairy Foods

1. Many kinds of foods use milk as an ingredient, such as yogurt, butter, and ice cream. Can you think of others? Bring several kinds of these foods to your meeting for a taste test. Which one is your favorite?

2. Try making some new flavors of yogurt. Get some plain, low-fat, or no-fat yogurt. Then, set out small bowls of different toppings: crunchy cereal, strawberries, bananas, peanut butter, blueberries, apple slices, nuts, honey, and other fruits. Have fun eating your unique dessert.

Some people are allergic to dairy foods. Maybe you are. Find out what kinds of substitutes can be used.

4. Food People

It is important to remember that "you are what you eat." Think about the foods you eat every day, using pictures of the healthy foods that are a part of your diet.

You will need:
• Construction paper.
• Pencil.
• Scissors.
• Glue.
• Crayons/markers.

1. On construction paper, draw pictures or paste ones from magazines of the foods you eat. Cut out the pictures, removing the unused paper.

2. Use the food shapes to create a person by gluing the cutouts of the food on a blank sheet of paper (see picture).

3. Share your food people with your friends.

5. Balancing Act

It is important to eat a well-balanced diet. You need to have at least 6 servings of grain, 3 servings of fruit, 4 servings of vegetables, 3 servings of protein, 3 servings of dairy, and very little fat and sugars.

Make a mobile representing the amount of different types of food you are supposed to eat every day.

You will need:
• 2 metal hangers.
• Construction paper.
• Crayons or markers.
• Tape.
• Yarn or string.
• Pencil.
• Glue.

1. On construction paper draw pictures (or use ones you cut out from magazines) of different foods that you eat based on the requirements found in the food pyramid.

2. Tape two hangers together at the top. Wrap yarn or string around the hangers until they are covered. Knot the end strings.

3. Use glue or tape to attach a string to each picture.

4. Tie the other end of the string to the covered hangers.

5. Hang your food pyramid mobile in a place where it will remind you each day about eating healthy foods.

GirlSports

To play sports it is important to learn the basics. Start by learning how to throw, catch, kick, volley, and strike.

1. Stretching Action

It is important to stretch before you exercise or play a sport and afterwards, too. Bending, twisting, and stretching your muscles will keep them flexible. Try these stretches. Hold each one about 20 seconds.

Thigh Stretch

1. Reach back and grab your left foot with your left hand.

2. Slowly pull your leg back so that your knee moves away from your body.

3. Feel the stretch in the front of your leg.

4. Repeat with your right leg.

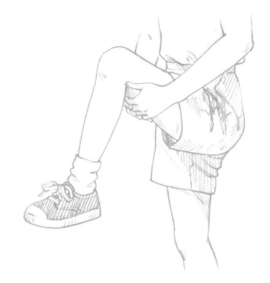

Back of Thigh Stretch

1. Place your hand under your left knee.

2. Pull your leg up.

3. You should feel a stretch down the back of your leg and your lower back.

4. Repeat this stretch with your right leg.

Try It!

Calf Stretch

1. Lean against a wall with your left leg behind you.

2. Keep your right knee slightly bent.

3. Lean forward until you feel a stretch in your calf.

4. Repeat with your right leg.

Chest and Shoulder Stretch

1. Bring both arms behind you with your fingers together.

2. Straighten your arms.

3. Lift your chest up.

Now that you have warmed up and stretched, it is time to make your heart and lungs stronger with aerobics. As your heart grows stronger, it takes less effort to do the same amount of work. Keep your heart pumping with one or two of the following activities: jumping rope, bicycling, or dancing.

V–Sit

1. Sit on the floor and make your legs into a "V".

2. Reach over and try to touch your right toes. Your knees can be slightly bent.

3. Then try to reach your left toes. Make sure you don't bounce.

4. Now lean forward and stretch your arms out in front of you.

Back Stretch

1. Lie on your back.

2. Bend your knees and bring them to your chest.

2. Throwing Skills

Practice underhand throwing using chalk and a beanbag.

• Make a circle on the ground with chalk.
• Stand about 5' back from the circle.
• Toss the beanbag into the circle.

Practice stepping forward with your opposite foot as you throw.

Now let's practice overhand throwing. You will need:

• Three 1-liter plastic soda bottles or milk jugs.
• Chalk or tape.
• 1 cardboard box.
• A beanbag.

1. Place the plastic bottles or milk jugs about 1" to 2" apart on the box. These will be your targets.

2. Use the chalk to draw a throwing line about 15' from the targets.

3. Stand behind the line and point at the targets with the hand that is not holding the beanbag.

4. If you are holding the beanbag in your right hand, step forward with your left foot. If you throw with your left hand, step forward with your right foot.

5. Extend your throwing arm, leading with your elbow.

6. Release the ball slightly above your head.

7. See how many bottles you can knock over in 5 throws.

3. Catching Practice

This activity builds on Activity #2, "Throwing Skills." You and your partner will need a beanbag.

1. Stand facing your partner. Make sure you stand far enough from your partner to be able to toss and catch the beanbag.

2. Practice throwing—remember to step forward with your left foot if you throw the beanbag with your right arm. Step forward with your right foot if you are left-handed.

3. After your partner catches the beanbag, she throws it back to you. Keep your hand cupped so you are ready to catch the beanbag.

4. Count how many times you and your partner can throw and catch the beanbag without dropping it.

4. Kicking Fun

Try kicking a large balloon in a safe, open play area.

1. Kick the balloon. Run to where it was kicked. Kick it again.

2. Kick the balloon so that it doesn't go very far from you. Tap lightly with the inside of your foot.

3. Kick the balloon with the inside of your foot.

4. Kick the balloon with the outside of your foot.

5. Kick the balloon so that it stays close to the ground.

6. Kick the balloon up into the air. Keep it off the ground. Kick with different parts of your foot.

7. Hold the balloon in both hands. Drop it and kick it before it hits the ground.

8. Kick back and forth with a partner.

5. Volleying

1. Hit a large balloon up in the air with your open hand. See if you can keep the balloon from hitting the ground.

2. Hit the balloon up with one hand, then the other. Keep it in the air. Hit it up above your head.

3. Reach up above your head. Hit the balloon upward with both hands. Use your fingertips. Keep the balloon above your head. Hit it again as it comes down.

4. Hit the balloon back and forth from one hand to the other.

5. Strike the balloon up into the air with your head.

6. Keep the balloon up in the air. Strike it with your head as it comes back down. Count how many times you can hit the balloon before it touches the ground.

7. Strike the balloon with different parts of your body—shoulder, elbow, knee, shin, thigh, chest, and foot.

6. Striking with a Paddle or a Racket

You will need:
• A paddle or racquet.
• A large balloon.

Follow these steps:
1. Hit the balloon with the paddle while standing in place.

2. Hit the balloon with the paddle while moving around.

3. Hit the balloon back and forth with a partner.

4. Hit the balloon high, hit the balloon low. Count how many times you and your partner hit the balloon before it hits the ground.

Healthy Habits

Exercise, rest, sleep, regular checkups, and cleanliness are all important to your health. Try the following activities to learn more about healthy living.

1. Community Helpers

Doctors, nurses, and dentists help you stay healthy. Visit one of them in your community and ask her or him to answer the following questions:

• How often should a young person go for a checkup?

• What special equipment is used?

• What can children do on their own to stay healthy?

• What do they like best about their jobs?

Try It!

2. Beautiful Smile

Keeping your teeth healthy is important. There are simple things you can do to help prevent cavities.

• The best time to brush is after meals. Brushing your teeth helps remove harmful germs.

• Get in the habit of flossing your teeth each day.

• Make regular visits to your dentist.

If you follow these three suggestions, you are doing a lot to help keep your teeth strong and your smile beautiful.

Practice brushing your teeth. Keep track of your progress with the chart below.

Teeth Cleaning Chart

	Morning	Evening	Floss
Sunday			
Monday			
Tuesday			
Wednesday			
Thursday			
Friday			
Saturday			

For every time you brush your teeth and floss, draw a smiling face in the box for that day. At the end of the week, count up your smiling faces. Compare your chart with your friends' charts to see who has the most smiling faces.

3. Calcium Counts

Calcium is important for building strong bones and teeth. Find the different foods that give your body the calcium it needs. You can form the words forward, backward, and diagonally up and down. The first one has been done for you.

For one week, write down how many times you eat food with calcium in it.

Word List:

~~Milk~~   ~~Broccoli~~   ~~Cheese~~
~~Spinach~~   ~~Yogurt~~   ~~Fish~~
~~Tofu~~   ~~Turnip~~   ~~Shrimp~~
~~Bok Choy~~ ~~Collard Greens~~

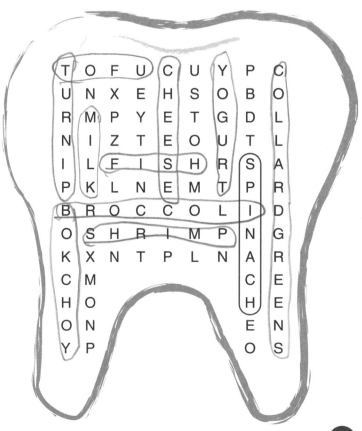

4. Smoking, a Bad Habit

Smoking is a very bad habit that can harm your health. Smoking damages your heart and lungs and makes it hard to breathe. Even being in the same room with someone who smokes can make you sick. See *Girl Scouts Against Smoking* to learn more about this harmful habit.

Maybe someone you really care about already smokes. It may be difficult to talk to her about this bad habit. One thing you can do is to ask her to do the activities in *Girl Scouts Against Smoking* with you. This may help her realize how much you care and how bad smoking can be.

Use the secret Brownie Girl Scout code below to figure out one message to share with people who might smoke.

Brownie Code

A ✳	B !	C 3	D 🌀
E 8	F ☺	G ?	H #
I 4	J ♡	K 2	L +
M ★	N 9	O %	P =
Q □	R 5	S 6	T ○
U 1	V ⊘	W △	X ❁
Y 7	Z ∝		

🌀% 9 ○ 6 ★ % 2 8
D o n 't   S m o k e !

5. Washing Works

Germs are all around us. They can spread from one person to another. They can make people sick.

You cannot see germs. If your hands look clean, that does not mean that they are clean. There may still be germs on your hands. Germs hide on both sides of your hands, in between your fingers, and under your fingernails.

It is important to wash your hands often to prevent the spread of germs. Washing your hands is one thing you can do to lower your chances of getting sick. Here are some good times to wash your hands:

- Before eating.
- Before setting the table and handling food.
- After going to the bathroom.
- After coughing or sneezing.

Here are the materials you will need:

- Soap.
- A sink with running water.
- Paper towels.

First teach yourself the hand-washing song.

"Washing Hands is Fun to Do"
(Sung to the tune of "Twinkle Twinkle Little Star")

Washing hands is fun to do
It keeps the germs off me and you
In our school or after play
We need to wash those germs away
After playing in the yard
Use some soap and scrub real hard

After you have learned the song it is time to practice washing your hands.

1. Turn on warm running water.

2. Get your hands soapy. Rub your hands together until you see soapy bubbles.

3. Wash both the front and back of your hands.

4. Remember to wash between your fingers and under your fingernails.

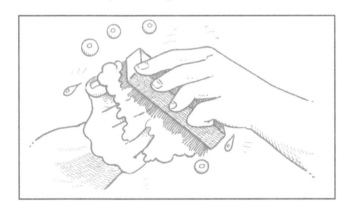

5. Rinse your hands under warm running water.

6. Dry your hands with a towel or paper towel. Use the towel to shut off the water so you don't get germs on your clean hands.

Tip: You should wash your hands for as long as it takes you to sing the song.

6. Feelings Game

How we deal with our feelings has an effect on our health.

You will need:
• A group of friends.
• A pack of index cards.
• Pencils.
• Crayons or markers.

1. Draw a picture on an index card that shows a feeling and write the word for that feeling underneath. The emotions on the card should include:

• Happy.	• Surprised.
• Sad.	• Embarrassed.
• Angry.	• Loving.
• Scared.	• Afraid.
• Excited.	• Upset.

2. After all the cards are completed, turn the pictures face down. The back of the cards should all look alike.

3. Mix up the cards while they are face down.

4. Decide who will go first. One at a time, pick up a card. Share with the group a time when you had that feeling.

5. Keep playing until no cards are left.

6. Shuffle the cards and start over again.

Try It!

Hobbies

A hobby is something you like to do when you have some free time. Hobbies can be collecting things, like coins or rocks; making things, like beaded jewelry or clay figures; or doing things, like reading or playing soccer.

1. Your Talents, Interests, and Hobbies

Most people start a hobby because they are interested in a topic or an activity or because they are good at doing something.

You are exploring many new things in Brownie Girl Scouts. Look through this book. What activities do you like the most? Make a list. Would these make good hobbies?

Before starting any hobby, you should ask yourself these questions. Then, talk about starting a hobby with your family.

	Yes	No
Do you think this hobby will be fun?	___	___
Can I afford this hobby?	___	___
Will I have space to do this hobby?	___	___
Will this hobby hurt the environment?	___	___
Is this hobby safe?	___	___
Do I have enough time for this hobby?	___	___

Discuss your answers with a parent or guardian.

2. Types of Hobbies

Make a list here of things you can collect:

. . . .

. . . .

. . . .

. . . .

Try It!

Maybe you have already begun a collection and don't even know it! Look around your home. Do you already have two or three or more things that can make a collection?

Make a list here of sports hobbies:

. . . .

. . . .

. . . .

. . . .

Make a list here of hobbies that involve making things:

. Chef . . . .

. artist . . . .

. sculpturist . . . .

. engineer . . . .

3. Organizing Your Hobby

If you are starting a collection, try organizing it. Give each thing a special label with its name and other important information. Arrange your collection to show it off. Your collection should be easy and attractive to see. If you can, go to a museum to see how collections of paintings, fossils, or dinosaur bones are arranged. Do the arrangements at the museum give you any ideas for organizing your own collection?

4. Practicing Your Hobby

Your hobby should give you lots of enjoyment, so make time for it. Once you have practiced your hobby for a while, try teaching it to a friend or family member.

Sunday _____

Monday_____

Tuesday_____

Wednesday_____

Thursday_____

Friday_____

Saturday_____

5. Making an Example

If your hobby is making things, like knitting, drawing, or building models, create and display an example to show other people how your craft is done.

6. Show and Tell

The other girls in your troop might choose hobbies very different from your own. Host a day of show and tell. Girls can describe their hobbies, display things they have made or collected, and help other girls get started with the same hobbies. You might invite a parent or guardian and your troop leader to show and tell their hobbies as well.

Make It, Eat It

While the most important reason to eat is because you need energy, food can also be a lot of fun to grow, prepare, and especially to eat.

1. Baked Apples

You will need:
- 1 baking apple for each person.
- 1/4 cup unsweetened apple juice for each apple.
- 2 tablespoons of raisins for each apple.
- 1 marshmallow for each apple.
- 1 teaspoon of ground cinnamon.
- A knife.

1. Have an adult help you peel the apple halfway down. Core the apple almost to its bottom.

2. Stuff the apple core with raisins.

3. Put the apple in a baking dish and pour the juice over it.

4. Sprinkle the apple with a little cinnamon.

5. Bake the apple in a 375ºF oven for 40-45 minutes. Put a marshmallow on top of the apple and let it melt.

6. Check that the apple is tender but not mushy.

7. Enjoy this treat hot or cold!

2. Fruit Fun

Prepare these recipes to serve at a get-together.

Fruit Juice Fizz

You will need:
- 1 orange or lemon.
- Orange juice.
- Pineapple juice.
- Cranberry juice.
- Seltzer or club soda.
- A pitcher.
- A knife.

1. Cut the orange or lemon into slices.

2. Put 1 or 2 cups of each juice into the pitcher.

3. For every 3 cups of juice, add 1 cup of seltzer. If you have 6 cups of juice, you need 2 cups of seltzer.

4. Add the slices of fruit.

5. Chill the juice.

6. Serve.

Fruit Salad

Take different types of fruit and cut them up into little pieces. Place all the fruit in a large bowl. Mix up the fruit. Serve the fruit in small cups with a topping of whipped cream.

3. Sloppy Joes

Make this recipe with your Girl Scout friends or your family. It is especially good when you make it outdoors! The recipe will serve 4-6 people. Ask an adult to help you.

You will need:
- 1 pound of ground beef or chicken.
- 1 can of tomato soup.
- Ketchup.
- Prepared mustard.
- Hamburger buns.
- Skillet.
- Container to hold excess fat.
- Strainer.
- Stove top, hot plate, or outdoor oven.

1. Brown the meat in the skillet.

2. Hold the strainer over the container for fat. Pour everything in the skillet into the strainer. It will catch the meat and let the fat run through.

3. Put the meat back in the skillet. Add the soup, ketchup, and mustard. Heat until thoroughly cooked.

4. Serve on the buns.

4. Green Thumb

Food does not just appear in the grocery store. Many of the products you eat have natural ingredients. Try this activity to see how fruits, vegetables, and herbs grow.

You will need:
• Seeds.
• Clay pots or other containers with holes in the bottom.
• Soil.
• Water.
• Spray bottle.
• Watering can.
• Plates.
• Masking tape.

1. Find a seed of a plant that you want to grow. Herbs and salad greens are the best for beginners.

2. Add soil to a clay pot (or other container) until it is almost full.

3. Push a seed under the soil with your finger. Read the back of the package to learn how deep to bury the seed. A seed that is buried too deep may not grow.

4. Do the same with four or five more seeds. Be sure there is some space between the seeds.

5. After you have planted the seeds, gently pat down the soil.

6. Place the pot on a plate. Carefully water the soil.

7. Write the name of the seeds you planted and the date, and tape the information on each pot.

8. Place the pot in an area that receives sunlight.

9. Check the soil every day. You need to keep the soil moist for the seeds to grow.

5. Recipe Book

You will need:
• A notebook.
• Magazines.
• Newspapers.
• Scissors.
• Glue.

1. Cut out pictures from magazines of different food products. Cut out letters from a newspaper that spell out the words "My Recipe Book." Glue the spelled-out words and the pictures onto the cover. Create any design you like.

2. Cover the book with a clear book cover or contact paper.

3. Divide the book into three sections: "Family Recipes," "Girl Scout Recipes," and "My Creations." Write the title on a blank page at the start of each new section. Decorate the section titles.

4. Add recipes that your friends and family have shared with you.

6. Brownie Soup

A Brownie Girl Scout needs her Brownie soup. Your Girl Scout friends can add their own ingredients to the basic recipe. Remember that an adult must be with you to be sure you're safe when cooking.

You will need:
• A can opener.
• A large spoon.
• A large pot.
• Bowls.
• Spoons.
• Ladle.
• 4 cups of broth (low-sodium is best).
• 3 cups of different kinds of vegetables.
• 1 cup of beans.
• 1/2 cup of rice.

1. Put the rice and 1 cup of water in the pot. Heat and stir.

2. When the rice is soft, add the vegetables, beans, and broth.

3. Heat until the soup is hot.

4. Serve.

5. Clean up.

Try It!

Me and My Shadow

A shadow is formed when a body or object blocks light. Artists study how light falls on things to create shadows. They use light in different ways in paintings, photographs, and other artwork.

1. Shadow Tag

Play a game of shadow tag. The girl who's "it" must tag someone else's shadow rather than the person. She can do this with her foot or use her own shadow. Think of ways you can keep your shadow out of trouble, besides running fast. Can you hide your shadow? How?

2. Tracing a Shadow

You will need:
• A partner.
• A lamp with no shade.
• A chair.
• Masking tape.
• Black marker or crayon.
• A large sheet of white paper.
• Magazines.
• Scissors.
• Glue.

1. Place a chair close to a wall with nothing hanging on it. Turn the chair sideways. Leave enough space for you to walk between the wall and the chair.

2. Have your partner sit in the chair. Walk about 20 steps from the chair. The lamp should be placed at the spot where you stopped. It needs to be on top of something that is as high as her head. The room should be dark except for the light from the lamp. Your partner's face and head should make a shadow on the wall. Tape the large sheet of paper to the wall where you see the shadow. Trace the outline of her face onto the paper. Cut out the face and fill it with a collage of magazine pictures that show things you like.

3. Shadow Animals

Point light from a lamp toward a blank wall. Using your hand, create different types of animal characters. Can you make a bird, a rabbit, or a dog? What others can you create?

With a friend or two, put on a skit with your shadow animals. Have the animals talk to each other or sing or make animal sounds.

4. Making Shadow-and-Light Plaques

You can make a plaque with your own interesting design.

You will need:
- A lightweight aluminum pan (like the ones frozen pies come in).
- A felt marker.

1. With a felt marker, draw a design on the pan.

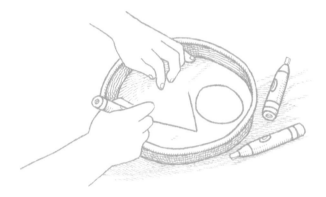

2. Put lots of newspaper on a table or counter so you don't damage its surface. Place the pan on the table or counter. With an adult's help, punch holes in the aluminum pan using a hammer and nails of different sizes.

3. Place your pan plaque against a window so that light can pass through the nail holes and highlight your design.

5. Shadow Box

Tell a favorite story in a shadow box.

You will need:
- A shoebox or other small box.
- Paper and cardboard.
- Glue.
- Tape.
- Scissors.
- Scraps of ribbon, fabric, pictures, and other materials.

Decorate the inside of your box to tell a scene from the story that you have chosen.

6. Shadow Display

Go outdoors and take pictures of shadows with a camera. An adult can explain how the camera works and help you load the film. Combine your photos with magazine photos and pictures that contain shadows to make a display of interesting shadows.

My Body

Try these fun activities to learn more about your body.

1. Brain Power

Try these activities to see how your brain works.

Different Muscles

Sit at a table and write your name. Then take one of your feet and move it in a circle on the floor. Now try doing both things together. Sometimes it's hard for your brain to do two things at once.

Eye to Brain to Hand

Cut a piece of paper the size of a dollar bill. Hold it in front of a friend. The idea is for your friend to have her hands in position to catch the piece of paper before it falls to the floor. Now let go of the piece of paper. What happened? Was your friend able to catch it?

The eyes send messages to the brain, which then tells the hands what to do. But sometimes an object falls faster than the message travels.

With your friend, practice this exercise. When your friend's skill at catching the falling piece of paper improves, switch roles.

2. Dreams

Your brain works even while you're sleeping—that's why you have dreams. In a circle with friends, tell about one of your dreams.

3. Funny Face

Muscles help you breathe, see, eat, and walk. Even your heart is a muscle. It pumps blood through your body. The more you exercise your muscles, the stronger they will grow.

Your face is full of different muscles. Looking into a mirror, make a frown. Make a happy face. Pretend to chew food or blow a bubble. Each change in expression is a result of your brain sending messages to the muscles in your face.

Your eyes also have muscles. Sit facing a friend. Keep your head still. Using just your eyes, look to the left, the right, up and down. The muscles in your eyes help move both of your eyes in the same direction even if your head is not moving.

Try It!

4. Body Volley

See how well you can use your muscles.

You will need:
• A balloon.
• A friend.

Facing your friend, you must try to keep the balloon in the air. Start by using your hands. Then one at a time, each of you calls out the name of a different part of your body. For example, if someone calls out "upper leg," you may only use your upper leg to keep the balloon in the air.

5. Muscle Reaction

Place one of your arms straight down by your side. Ask a friend to hold your arm down while you try as hard as you can to lift it. Count to 20, trying as hard as you can to lift your arm. After you have counted to 20, your friend can let go. Stand still and let your arm relax. What does your arm do? Why do you think this happens?

6. Pulse

Your heart pumps blood through the body. Every time your heart beats, it pushes a new supply of blood through your body. Arteries are the tubes that carry blood away from your heart. You can feel the blood going through your arteries when you take your pulse.

Now try to find your pulse on your wrist. Hold your finger as the diagram shows. Remember not to use your thumb in checking a pulse. Your thumb has a pulse of its own.

Now take a friend's pulse on her wrist.

Check your pulse after you have run around or played a game for a little while. Has your pulse rate gone up or down? Why?

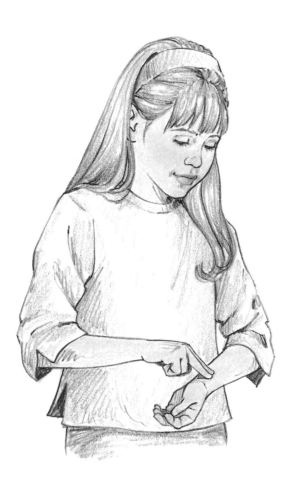

7. A Fit Body

Look at the fitness wheel in the picture and then make one of your own.

You will need:
- Heavy cardboard.
- Scissors.
- Crayons or markers.

1. Cut a piece of heavy cardboard into a circle.

2. Draw four straight lines through the middle of the circle. Use different colors. You should have eight spaces in which to write the names of exercises.

Here are some ideas for exercises you can do:
- Hopping.
- Galloping.
- Skipping.
- Frog jumps.
- Crab crawl.
- High knees.
- Sliding.
- Dancing.

3. Close your eyes and point to the wheel and do the exercise you picked.

8. Body Parts

Your body has many parts that work together. Choose a friend and trace an outline of each other's bodies on paper.

You will need:
• Butcher paper or other long pieces of paper.
• Pencils.
• 13 paper fasteners for each girl.
• Scissors.
• A partner.

1. Take turns tracing each other's body on the paper.

2. Cut around the body that was drawn.

3. Cut the body apart at the neck, shoulders, elbows, wrists, thighs, knees, and ankles (see the picture).

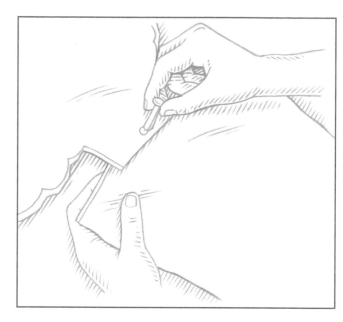

5. Label the different body parts. Also draw the eyes, nose, ears, mouth, and hair.

6. Sign each body puppet with your handprint and your name.

7. Display your "body puppets" around the room.

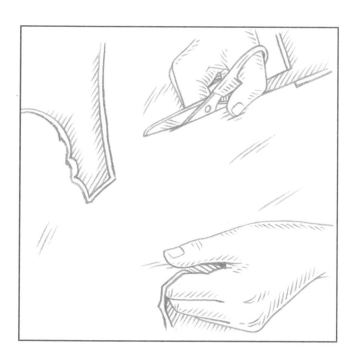

4. Fasten the body parts back together with the paper fasteners. You now have moving body parts, like parts of a puppet.

Penny Power

Save it, spend it, earn it, borrow it, donate it. Money is an important part of everyone's life. Start now to learn the basics of dealing with money.

1. Cookie Dough

With your troop, write a plan for using the money you earn from the Girl Scout Cookie Sale. (Remember that you may not sell Girl Scout Cookies on the Internet.)

2. Is It Real?

Counterfeit money is fake money, and it is a serious problem in this country. The colored bills that you may find in a favorite board game are not the problem. Everyone knows that these bills are "pretend" money. The fake money that some criminals make look like real bills. But there are important differences. Find out how the new $5 and $10 bills that are made by the U.S. Department of the Treasury can prevent people from using fake money. Ask an adult what you should do if you are given a bill that is not real.

3. Bank on It

Most banks are interested in helping children get into the habit of saving. Visit your local bank and find out what you need to do to open a savings account.

4. The Price You Pay

Set up a "pretend" store and practice making change. Put price tags on items that you are selling. Set your prices from one penny to one dollar. Your friends can be the customers. They can use pennies, nickels, dimes, quarters, and dollar bills (real or ones you've made) to buy these products. You can give change to your customers. Then change roles so that you have an opportunity to buy and your friends can be the storeowners.

Try It!

5. Step Right Up!

Set up a tag sale with your troop or friends. You can each contribute toys or books you no longer need. Work together with your Girl Scout leader or other adults to set prices and make signs. After the sale, discuss why certain types of items sold well while others did not. Add the money you make to your troop funds.

6. Keeping Tabs

Keep track of how much money you use each week. How much do you spend at lunchtime? On treats or toys? For phone calls? If you get an allowance, is it enough for all of these things? If you don't, how much allowance would you need? Think of a way that you could save some part of your real or imaginary allowance.

Safety Sense

Every Girl Scout knows the motto "Be Prepared." Read pages 62–75 in the *Brownie Girl Scout Handbook* about safety and try these activities.

1. Street Safety

Make a map of your neighborhood and mark the places you need to know about, like the police station and firehouse, to stay safe. Or use a map and mark the important places.

2. Fire Safety Practice

Read the section on fire safety on pages 66–67 in your handbook. Find out about the fire escape plan for your Brownie Girl Scout meeting place and practice it. Design a backup plan that can be used if the first way out is blocked.

3. Smoke Alarm

Having a working smoke alarm is an important part of fire safety.

1. Learn what a smoke alarm is and how it works. If there is no smoke alarm in your home, talk to an adult in your family about why it's important to get one.

2. If you have a smoke alarm, have an adult test it so you can hear what it sounds like. Discuss what you should do when you hear the alarm.

4. Playground Safety

Playgrounds are great places to have fun. You can swing, jump, run, and hang by your legs. But they can also be dangerous if you are not careful. What are some rules that you can use to make sure playgrounds are safe? Talk with your Girl Scout leader and troop about your ideas. Afterward, make a poster illustrating these safety rules.

5. First Aid

Learn a skill that could save a life in an emergency. For example, many people do choke while eating. You can tell if a person is in trouble if she can't talk or cough, if she points to her mouth or holds her neck, or if she is turning blue. With an adult, learn a first-aid technique for choking.

Pretend your partner is choking. Keep her calm. Ask her to cough. If she cannot breathe, cough, or speak:

1. Stand behind her.

2. Make a fist with one hand and place it above her belly button, just below the rib cage.

3. Grasp the fist with the other hand.

4. Then push your fist in and up quickly. Be sure when you're practicing not to push hard on the person's stomach.

5. Keep doing this until she can spit out the object and can breathe and speak.

Practice first aid for choking on yourself so you'll be prepared in case there is a time when no one can help you.

6. Safety Center

Make a place to keep information you'll need in an emergency.

You will need:
• A hanger.
• A piece of oak tag that is the same width as the hanger.
• Glue.
• Markers.
• At least 3 envelopes.

1. Wrap one end of the oak tag around the hanger and glue it.

2. With a marker, label the envelopes. A few ideas are:

• Small change.

• Emergency phone numbers.

• Reminder notes.

Include an envelope in which to keep paper and a pencil for taking messages.

3. Glue each envelope to the oak tag. Hang it near the phone for you to reach easily.

If you'd like, you can substitute felt for the oak tag.

Try It!

Sports and Games

Sports and games are a great way to give your body exercise, to make friends, and to learn how to work with other girls and have fun.

1. Skating

Ice skating and roller skating are fun sports and are good for fitness. Always skate with a buddy and follow safety rules.

You will need:
- A pair of skates.
- Comfortable clothes.
- Safety items—kneepads, elbow pads, wrist guards, helmet.

Find a flat, open, and safe area to practice these skills.

1. Practice falling. Standing still, bend your knees and lean forward. Fall forward so that your kneepads hit the floor first. Extend your arms in front of you, using your wrist and elbow guards to help soften the fall. You should also practice falling while moving at slow speeds. Remember to keep your body relaxed and loose. If you stiffen up when you fall, you increase your chance for injury.

2. Practice stopping. The right technique will depend on the type of skates you are using.

3. Practice skating forward. Skate to the left and to the right. If you are a more advanced skater, you can try this skill backwards.

2. Bicycling

Try these bicycling skills.

1. Ride as slowly as you can without stopping.

2. Ride in circles. Try to make the circles as small as you can.

3. Ride in a long, straight line.

4. Practice turning, using hand signals. To turn left, put your left arm straight out with the palm forward. To turn right, put your left arm out and bent upward at the elbow, with fingers pointing up. To stop, put your left arm out and bent down at the elbow, with fingers pointing down.

5. Set up a bicycling practice course. Place about 10 large metal cans in a wide play area. Try to ride around the course without touching the cans.

3. Swimming

Have an adult teach you how to swim. Always remember the following rules:

• Have an adult watch you.

• Swim with a buddy.

• Swim where there is a lifeguard with rescue equipment.

• Leave the water before you get tired or cold.

Ask an adult to help you practice:

1. *Blowing bubbles.* Take a deep breath and place your face in the water. Blow the air out. You should see bubbles.

2. *Bobbing in the water.* Hold an adult's hand in water up to your chest. Take a breath. Bend your knees and as your head goes under the water, slowly breathe out. Then straighten your legs and return to the surface. Remember, when your face is above the water, you breathe in. When it is below the water, you breathe out.

3. *Holding your breath.* Hold an adult's hand while in the water. Take a deep breath. Next, place your face in the water. See how many seconds you can hold your breath.

4. Games

Look through your handbook or other books for several games to play. Choose two games to play with your friends and teach a third game to someone else.

5. Octopus Tag

Working together is very important in sports and games. Try this game with your friends.

You will need:

• A safe place with clear boundaries.

• At least 4 people.

1. Pick one person to be the octopus. Have everyone who is playing line up together on one side.

2. The octopus begins the game by shouting "feeding time."

3. Everyone tries to run to the safe place without getting tagged. If the person gets caught, she must now hold hands with the octopus.

4. Now the two people become the octopus. They must hold hands and work together. After shouting "feeding time," they must run together and try to tag more people.

5. When someone else is caught, she also becomes part of the octopus. Continue the game until everyone has been tagged.

Try It!

53

Write Away

Writing and its good friend reading are two terrific activities. If you are feeling bored or lonely or feel like doing a quiet activity, reading a good book can introduce you to exciting adventures. Telling your own story can also be fun. You make up characters and have them act in any way that you choose. Grab a pencil and paper or a book, magazine, or newspaper and "try-it" yourself!

1. All About Me

Write a story about your life (this is called an autobiography). You might want to describe your family, your home, your hobbies, your pets, your friends, your favorite activities, the things you like to eat or wear, and anything else that is important to you. Try illustrating your autobiography. You can draw pictures, or you can use photographs.

2. Read the Story of Someone Special

Many books have been written about famous people. These are called biographies. Choose one to read. You might want to read about Juliette Gordon Low or Jackie Joyner-Kersee or Helen Keller or Harriet Tubman.

Once upon a time an eight-year-old girl lived in a 15-story building. Her baby brother ...amed Kurt and her ...amed Tucker

3. Group Giggles

To do this activity you will need at least two or three other people. Have one girl start the story. She might say, for example, "I skipped through a field full of flowers in all the colors of the rainbow when all of a sudden . . . ." Another person continues the story. Keep going until everyone has had a chance to add her part and the story is done.

4. Become a Reporter

Many times, people who write articles for newspapers or magazines do interviews. They get to meet interesting and sometimes famous people. Interview someone you know and try to find out one particularly unusual fact about her or him. You might, for example, discover that your school bus driver plays the tuba or that your teacher has six sisters. Prepare about five questions, and keep asking until you find out one really fun fact.

5. Write a Letter

Staying in touch with friends who move away or ones you meet at summer camp or on vacation can be difficult. But writing can help. Write letters that you send either through regular mail or e-mail. Tell your friends all about the Try-Its you are earning and the other things you are doing.

OR

Check out the Girls Only Web site (www.gogirlsonly.org). Ask for advice on a problem that has really been bugging you. (Keep in mind that Dr. M can only answer a question a week from the hundreds she receives.) See if there is any place asking for you to write something, and then just try it.

6. Like It or Not

Read your favorite magazine. Which articles did you like best and which did you find boring? Why did you like some and not others? Was it the topic? The way it was written? Did some include activities that you enjoyed doing? Do the same things with the ads in the magazine.

Share the magazine with a friend and find out whether your likes or dislikes are similar.

Try It!

3

Family
and Friends

All In the Family

Your family is made up of the people you live with, learn from, have fun with, help, and love. And they help and love you, too.

1. Where Are You From?

Find out about your family background. Did your family come from another state? Did either of your parents, your grandparents, or your great-grandparents come from another country? Look at a map or globe and find that country.

Are any of your ancesters American Indian? Which Indian nation? What area did it cover?

Share a family story, tradition, dance, or a type of food with others in your Girl Scout troop.

2. Say Cheese

Take a photograph of your family or make a family picture. The picture can:

• Show people in your family.

• Express a feeling.

• Show a family event.

Have a "Family Night" art show with your Girl Scout troop or group. Invite everyone's family to the exhibit!

3. Coupon Collection

Make a "gift coupon" for everyone in your family. For example, make one for your mom or dad that says, "I'll clear the dinner dishes for one week" or "I'll clean my room without being asked." Then distribute the coupons and be sure to carry out what you wrote.

4. Birthday Countdown

You can make a birthday poster as a gift for a family member's birthday.

You will need:
• Poster paper or cardboard.
• Pencil.
• Glue.
• Scissors.
• Long pieces of thick yarn.
• Old magazine pictures of things the birthday person likes.

1. Using glue, write the age that the person will be on paper or cardboard.

2. Place the yarn on top of the glue.

3. Cut out pictures of things that the birthday person likes.

4. Glue the pictures around the number.

5. Family Fitness

Help your family become more fit. Do any of the following activities. The more you do, the healthier everyone will be.

• Help plan and make a healthy meal for your family.

• See who in your family can jump the highest. The farthest. The fastest. Keep a stretch the longest.

• Go on a family fun run! Walk, skip, dance, or run one quarter of a mile with someone in your family.

6. Make a Family Time Capsule

Time capsules capture a point in time. People can look at a time capsule to see what real people were like in the past. Your time capsule will capture a picture of you and your family now, so you'll remember years from now what you were like when you were a Brownie Girl Scout.

You will need:
• A container.
• Paper.
• Pencils.
• Magazines.
• Scissors.
• Souvenirs.

1. Find photographs or illustrations in magazines that relate to some of the interests of members of your family. Before cutting out the pictures from the magazines, get permission from a parent or guardian. Label the back of each picture. For example, if your dad likes to draw, write "Dad loves to draw" on the back of a picture of colored pencils.

2. Roll up the pictures and place them in your container—this is your time capsule.

3. Decorate the outside of the time capsule. Put today's date on it.

4. Hide the container somewhere in your home. Make a record of the hiding place so you don't forget where it is. After five years, open your time capsule. You may be surprised at the memories and feelings you experience as you look at the record of your family's past.

Caring and Sharing

No one in the world is exactly like you—or your friends! Show how you care about yourself and others with these activities.

1. I Care

Be a "secret pal" to someone. Think of nice things you can do for your secret pal. Write a poem, make a friendship pin, send a card, or be a helper.

2. Favorites

Make a list of some of your favorites—songs, books, places, things to do. Compare your list with your friends' lists. What things are the same? Different? Try reading a friend's favorite book or watching a friend's favorite movie with her. Ask her why she likes it.

_____

_____

_____

_____

_____

3. What If?

With your Girl Scout troop or group, talk about what makes a person a good friend. How can you be a good friend to another person? With your Brownie Girl Scout friends, act out what you would do in two of the following situations:

• Your best friend is crying.

• One of the girls in the troop has a birthday.

• Your mother has to finish a big project for work the next day.

• A neighbor falls and breaks her leg.

• Your friend is afraid she will fail a test.

• A classmate forgot her lunch.

Think of other scenes to act out.

Try It!

4. Differences Are OK

Many people look different from you. Some have skin or hair that is another color. Some are taller or shorter. One person may see better and another not hear as well. All these people have similar feelings on the inside. They also have talents to share.

With your Girl Scout troop or group, find out about ways that you are different from each other. Find out about ways you are the same as others. Choose a partner and stand or sit facing her:

1. Interview your partner. Ask her about her family, where she lives, and her favorite food, activity, and movie. Then your partner gets a turn to find out about you.

2. Come together as a group and talk about some of the ways you are different and the same.

5. A Friend's Scrapbook

Make a scrapbook that tells about your friends.

You will need:
• Construction paper.
• Writing paper.
• A stapler.
• Markers or crayons.
• A pencil.

1. Fold the construction paper in half. This will be the cover.

2. Decide how many friends you want to put in your book. Make a page for each of them.

3. Staple the pages and cover together.

4. Decorate the cover.

5. Make a page for each friend. You may want to put in pictures, phone numbers, birthdays, addresses, or other things you think would be fun.

6. Be a Good Neighbor

Is there a neighbor who needs your help? Is she busy with kids? Or taking care of someone elderly? Or is she elderly herself? Find out what is needed and help out! You could share conversation, weed a garden, or do a chore. Be sure you have permission from your parent or guardian.

Friends Are Fun

In Girl Scouting you make new friends and learn to strengthen the friendships you already have.

1. Make New Friends...

Look for new friends at school or at after-school activities. Is there someone who is sitting by herself? Does she look lonely? Go up, smile, and introduce yourself. Then invite her to join you!

2. Friendship Bracelet

Celebrate with a friendship bracelet. Give it as a gift, or make matching ones for your friends and yourself!

You will need:
- A cardboard tube.
- Scissors.
- Thin yarn in 3 or 4 different colors.
- Tape.
- Pencil.

Try It!

1. Take the cardboard tube and carefully cut it open lengthwise.

2. Place the tube on your wrist and mark off how wide you want the bracelet to be.

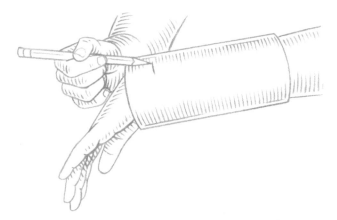

3. Remove the tube from your arm and cut the tube to that width.

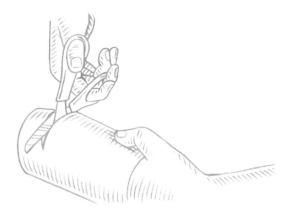

4. Cover the inside of the tube with tape. This will help keep the bracelet's shape.

5. Tape a piece of yarn to the back of the cardboard. Wind one color of yarn over and over the cardboard. Be sure that you cover up the tape on the back of the tube.

6. Use as much of one color as you want, then cut the yarn, making sure to leave a "tail."

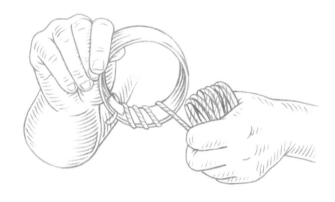

7. Start your next color. It should overlap a bit with your first color. See the picture.

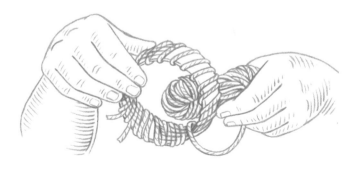

8. Continue this with other colored yarns until the bracelet is completely covered. Weave the end through the yarns on the back of the bracelet to secure it.

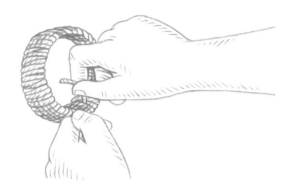

9. Cut all remaining yarn "tails."

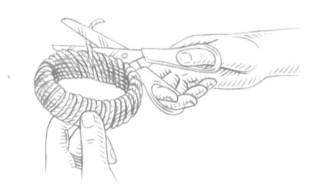

You can use this same technique on headbands and picture frames, too! Or you can create special pencils for you and your friends to use to write to each other.

3. Paper Design

Make colorful writing paper and matching envelopes for keeping in touch with a special friend.

You will need:
- Pencils.
- Rubber stamps and ink pad.
- Colored pencils or markers.
- Ruler.
- Plain paper and envelopes.

1. Using the ruler, measure off 1" from all edges of the paper. Make light dots every couple of inches along each edge. Using the straight edge of the ruler, connect the dots. You've now made a light border around the paper. This is the area you'll decorate.

2. Use rubber stamps or colored markers and pencils to create a design along the border. Duplicate this design on your envelopes.

4. Create a Code

Have you ever gotten a secret message? Making and cracking codes is fun! Here's an "alphabet soup" code to try with a friend:

1. Write out the alphabet on a piece of paper. Leave room under each letter to write a number or draw a picture. That's your code!

2. Write out the message you want to send to your friend.

3. Now substitute the number or picture that's under each letter of your message.

4. Rewrite your message using only the numbers and/or pictures.

5. Pass your message on to your friend. Make sure she has a copy of the decoding sheet or she won't be able to read the message.

5. Measure Up!

You and a friend can send secret messages to each other, using this technique. Make sure you have the same size rulers or you won't be able to read what she's written.

You will need:
- 2 rulers of equal length.
- Scissors.
- Marker or pencil.
- Tape.
- Paper.

1. Cut a strip of paper 1" across and about 2 1/2 times as long as your ruler.

2. Tape one end of the paper to the end of the ruler as shown on page 65.

3. Carefully wrap the paper strip around the ruler as shown below.

4. Write a short message on the paper, across the front of the ruler. Make sure to mark the beginning of the message with a star.

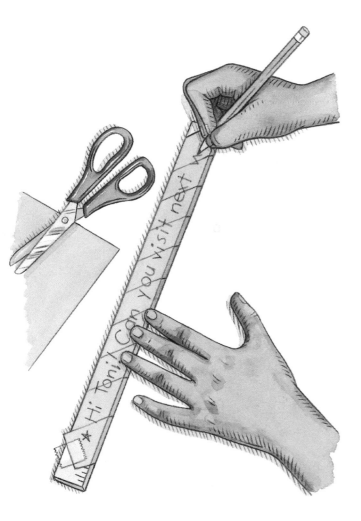

5. Carefully unwrap the paper and send it to your friend. She will wrap the paper around her ruler, beginning with the part that's marked with a star.

6. Flower Power

Did you know that over the years some flowers have come to have a special meaning? Did you know that we give red roses to a friend as a way of saying we love her? Or that forget-me-nots represent remembering?

The chrysanthemum is a flower that stands for friendship. Celebrate one of your friendships by planting a chrysanthemum in a pot. As your friendship grows, so will the flower!

You will need:
• A flowerpot with a drainage hole and a saucer.
• Dirt.
• Chrysanthemum seeds.
• A watering can or cup.
• A stick.
• Small pebbles.

1. Line the bottom of the flowerpot with pebbles.

2. Fill the rest of the pot with dirt.

3. Make two 2" holes in the dirt with a stick. Your holes should be 2" apart from each other. Place a seed in each hole.

4. Lightly cover each seed with dirt. Gently water the seeds and dirt until the water seeps out the bottom of the pot and onto the saucer.

5. Keep your plant in the sunshine and follow the directions on the seed package for watering. In a short time, you'll have a couple of chrysanthemum plants. Give one to your friend for her to transplant!

Let's Pretend

Movies, stories, television shows, songs, and even dances are often based on "make-believe." When you pretend to be someone or something you're not, you're "acting." Go onstage with some of these activities.

1. Be a Mime

A *mime* acts out a story without using any sounds or words. Using the list below, mime three simple situations. See if others can guess what you are miming!

• Without words, act out three different daily activities like making your bed, feeding the dog, reading a book.

• Pick up an imaginary object. What shape is it? How heavy is it? What does it smell like? Pass it to another person. Careful! You don't want it to fall and break!

• Create a setting by acting out one of these scenes. Or try one of your own!

— A bird inside a bird cage.
— Someone learning to play a musical instrument.
— Toasting a marshmallow over a camp fire on a cold night.

2. If You Were....

With four or more friends, work together to become a type of machine. Together you can be:

• A train.
• A computer.
• A washing machine or dryer.

Be sure to add movement and sound to your machine as you make it work.

3. Dress It Up

Gather together bedsheets, old clothes, coats, towels, hats, Halloween wigs, and other things you have permission to use. Make and then try on different outfits. How do they make you feel? Can you act differently in these outfits than you do in your everyday clothes?

4. Act It Out

As a group, pick one fairy tale, fable, or well-known story. Act out the main scenes from that story. You can use costumes, props, and set pieces if you want. Perform the scenes for your families and friends.

5. Louder, Please!

Try these two breathing exercises to help make sure you're heard in the back row.

• Put your hands on your waist. As you breathe in, your waist should get bigger, pushing against your hands. As you breathe out, your waist should get smaller. Say "Ahhh" as you breathe out. How long can you hold that "Ahhh"? Have a friend time you.

• Rest for a minute. Do the same exercise, but this time see how loudly you can say "Ahhh." How loudly can your friend do it?

6. Tongue Twisters

You have to speak clearly if you want to be understood. Try each of the following tongue twisters slowly at first. Then try to say them faster and faster. How many times in a row can you say them? How quickly can you say them?

• Rubber baby buggy bumper.
• She sells sea shells by the sea shore.
• Toy boat.

Make up one of your own tongue twisters. Share it with a friend.

7. Putting Your Best Face Forward

Masks are sometimes used in plays, dances, and festivals. They can be just a decoration or part of a costume.

You will need:
• Paper plate (8"-10" round).
• Elastic cord.
• Markers and crayons.
• Glue.
• Fabric, ribbon, and other decorations.
• Scissors.

1. Cut the paper plate in half. Use one of these halves for your mask.

2. Hold the plate half up to your face. The round part should be up and the straight part down. With your fingers, feel along the plate until you come to the place where your eyes are. Using a crayon, mark this spot.

3. Carefully cut circles in the spot that you marked for your eyes.

4. Between and below your eyes, cut a little space for your nose.

5. Decorate your mask, using crayons, markers, ribbon, or fabric.

6. Make a small hole at each side of your mask. Thread the elastic through the holes and make knots to keep it in place.

Try It!

Manners

Whether you are meeting new people or are with your family and friends, good manners are important.

1. Respect for Others

Showing respect for others means treating them the way you want to be treated. Part of the Girl Scout Law states, "I will do my best to respect myself and others."

Think of ways you can show respect for others. Discuss with your troop or group and your family how you can respond when people are not respectful toward you. With others, create a song, skit, or poem about respect.

2. Meeting People

Making polite introductions is part of having good manners. Introductions may be different from one culture to the next.

1. Practice introducing yourself to others in your troop, at home, and in school. Include a smile, a handshake, and a friendly greeting. Say something like "Hi, my name is…."

2. Practice introducing other people. Introductions are made in a certain order. The common rule is that you say an older person's name first, as well as the name of people with important positions or titles. For example, you would say, "Ms. Lewis, I'd like you to meet Alexis Smith. Alexis, this is Ms. Lewis."

Practice these introductions:

- A new girl in your troop.
- A friend to a parent.
- A person with a special title or degree, such as father, rabbi, doctor, or judge. Try using a person's job title—for example, "Hello, Dr. Jones, I am…."

3. All Around the World

Practice these greetings used in different parts of the world:

- In Japan, a bow is a traditional greeting.
- In Chile, a handshake and a kiss to the right cheek are customary.
- In Fiji, a smile and an upward movement of the eyebrows are how people greet one another.

Learn titles that are used in other languages and cultures. For example, "Señora" is the Spanish title for a married woman. In Japan,

"San" is used after someone's name to show respect for the person. In Turkey, an older woman calls a younger woman "Canim," which means "dear" or "beloved." In this country, Navajo people use the term "Hosteen," which means uncle, for older men they admire.

Find out how to say "please" and "thank you" in another language.

4. Table Manners

Pretend you are at a restaurant. Talk with your friends about polite and impolite ways to act. Take turns being the waiter and the customer. You can have even more fun by using sample menus from restaurants and a place setting (plates, cups, silverware) for each person.

5. Eating Customs

Good table manners in the United States may not be good manners to a Girl Guide from India or Japan. Did you know that many cultures use tableware different from a knife and fork and spoon? In some cultures you might find people using chopsticks. In some cultures, people eat with their fingers. You might also find different table settings or no table at all. Learn about some ways people in other cultures eat.

With your troop, plan to serve a snack where you can use different table manners, utensils, or seating.

6. Phone Fun

Practice telephone manners. In pairs, act out some conversations.

1. There's an emergency at home and you need to call for help.

2. Someone from your mother's workplace wants to leave a message.

3. Your grandmother calls you to chat.

7. Hosting a Party

Host a party with your troop to celebrate an accomplishment, a holiday, or a birthday, or just because you want to. Discuss how guests at a party should act. Put these ideas into action when you're a guest at a party.

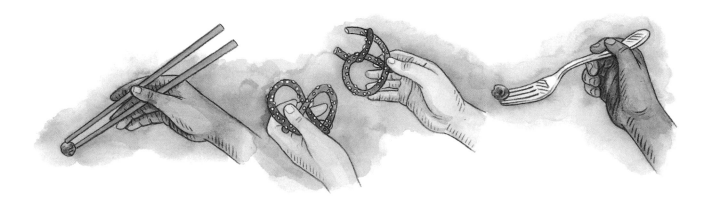

People Are Talking

People communicate not only with words but in other ways, too. Your tone of voice, how you say something, how you stand, and where you place your eyes will help you get your message across.

1. It's Not What You Say, But How You Say It

Say the following lines to a partner. Then say the same lines in a different way. Ask your partner if she hears a difference. Have her explain what the difference is.

Switch roles. Listen carefully to your partner as she says the lines in different tones of voice. Tell her what you thought she was saying each time she spoke the lines. Then ask her what she was trying to say.

- "You're my best friend."
- "Do you want to come to my slumber party?"
- "You want to be my friend?"
- "I'm sorry."

2. Body Language

Your body has a language all its own. Watch a couple of television programs without the sound on. Can you tell what people are feeling? Who's happy? Who's angry? Who's lying? How can you tell?

3. Getting the Feel of Things

Play "Guess the Feeling." In a bowl, place scraps of paper with different feelings written on them (for example, "excited" or "angry"). Take turns picking a piece of paper. Without using any sounds or words, try to express the emotion on the paper to the rest of the group. Then try to show the feeling using only part of your body: your head, your hands, or your eyes.

4. Do You Really Care?

A good listener is an active listener. She's someone who looks like she really cares what people are talking about. How does she do that? She:

• Looks right at the person who is talking.
• Doesn't get distracted by other sounds or actions.
• Doesn't interrupt.
• Asks questions.

Practice being a good listener with your Girl Scout troop. Sit in pairs. One girl tells a story. The other girl practices the above skills. Then switch. What did it feel like when you told your story to someone who was really listening to you? Was it hard to be an active listener?

5. Different Languages

English is our national language in the United States, but in many other countries people speak languages that sound foreign to us. Find out how to say three words or phrases in another language. What do the words or phrases mean?

6. Become Handy

Look at the sign language alphabet on pages 86-87 of the *Brownie Girl Scout Handbook*. Learn how to spell your name using sign language. Learn two phrases in sign language. Teach them to a friend.

Puppets, Dolls, and Plays

You are learning about many kinds of art, such as painting and sculpture. Did you know that making puppets and dolls is an art, too? You can use them in plays or stories.

1. Finger Puppets

Turn the fingers of a glove into little puppets. Then put on a play.

You will need:
• An old cloth or knitted glove.
• Piece of ribbon.
• String.
• Thread.
• Yarn.
• Glue.
• Scraps of old material.
• Markers.
• Small buttons.
• Beads.
• Tissue paper.

Try It!

1. Make five grape-sized balls with the tissue paper, and stuff one into each finger of the glove.

2. Tie a piece of ribbon or yarn on the outside of the glove and under the tissue ball.

3. Make a face on each fingertip with the markers, or sew or glue on buttons or beads.

4. Glue threads or yarn on the tip of the finger for hair.

5. Use yarn and scraps of cloth to dress your puppet.

6. Tell a story using your finger puppets.

2. Yarn Doll

Have fun putting a yarn doll together.

You will need:
- Yarn or heavy thread.
- A small ball, a small round pebble, or a small ball of yarn.
- Ribbons.
- Cloth scraps.
- Buttons.
- Other materials you like.

1. Cut the yarn into strips the length of this page.

2. Make enough strips to fill your hand.

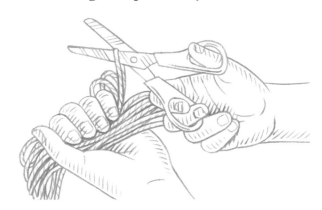

3. Tie all the strips together at the top.

4. Insert a Ping-Pong ball, pebble, or small ball of yarn to give shape to the head.

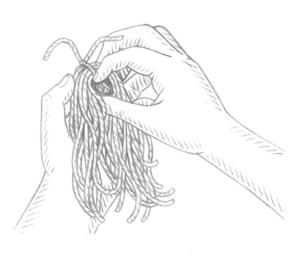

5. Tie another string to the bottom of the ball to make a neck.

6. Make arms and legs and a waist, as in the drawing.

7. Use cloth and ribbons to dress the doll.

3. Paper-Bag Puppet

Use a paper bag to make an animal puppet.

You will need:
- Small paper bags.
- Pieces of paper.
- Crayons.
- Markers or paint.
- Scissors.
- Glue.

1. Place the paper bag flat on a table with the bottom fold on top.

2. Draw and color designs on the bottom fold of the bag. This will be the head of your puppet. You can add eyes, ears, and hair.

3. Decorate the rest of the bag. What did you make?

4. Marionette

A marionette is a puppet that dangles from strings. You can make just about any marionette figure from cardboard.

You will need:
- A couple of sheets of heavy paper (for body and head).
- A sheet of cardboard (for crosspieces).
- Scissors.
- Paper fasteners (brads).
- String.
- Hole puncher.

1. Cut out a head, a body, arms, and legs from the cardboard. Cut two parts for each leg and two for each arm.

2. Use the hole puncher to make holes in each piece before you connect them with the paper fasteners. Where you connect the two parts of the leg is the "knee." Where you connect the two parts of the arm is the "elbow." Make sure the holes are big enough to allow the arms and legs to move easily.

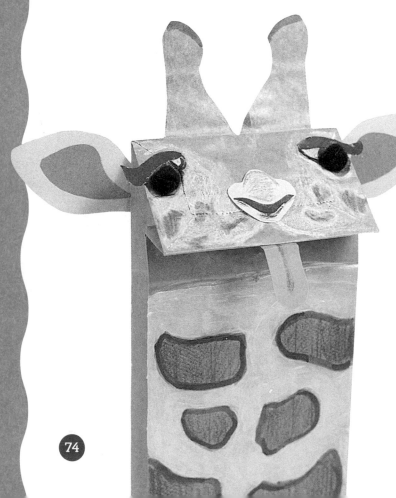

Try It!

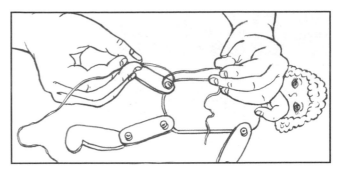

8. Thread the string through the holes in the crosspieces and knot them so they don't fall out. Add one more string from the head to the crosspiece. Cover with the paper fastener.

9. Hold the crosspiece in one hand and pull on the strings with the other. Your marionette should move easily.

10. Color in your marionette. Or dress it in paper doll clothes or fabric.

5. A Puppet Stage

A stage will make a puppet show much more fun. A puppet stage will have three parts— the stage itself, a curtain, and scenery.

Try using a box, a table, or chairs for the stage, and a sheet, a towel, or a tablecloth for the curtain. What can you use for scenery? Look around your home or meeting place, or cut out some shapes from heavy cardboard.

6. Safety Play

Read about safety on pages 62-69 in the *Brownie Girl Scout Handbook*. Create a puppet show about safety do's and don'ts.

3. Fasten the parts together with the paper fasteners.

4. Cut out two crosspieces from the cardboard.

5. Use the hole puncher to make a hole in the center of each crosspiece.

6. Connect them with a paper fastener.

7. Attach lengths of string from the paper fasteners at the marionette's "knees" and "elbows." Make sure that the string is long enough to allow the marionette to move. (The string for the knees should be twice as long as the string for the elbows).

Stitch It Together

If you can sew, you can do basic things like attach a button, fix a hem, or repair a tear. You can also learn to make clothes and even costumes for plays. It's also fun to learn a skill like embroidery, and to be able to make decorations for your home.

1. Animal Sewing Card

You will need:
- Large magazine pictures.
- Colored yarn.
- Glue stick.
- Cardboard.
- Hole puncher.
- Tape.

1. Cut out a large picture of an animal.

2. Glue or tape this picture onto a piece of cardboard.

3. With an adult's help, punch holes outlining the animal. If you want, add more holes for its eyes, paws, whiskers, etc.

4. Tape one end of the yarn to the back of the card. Wrap the other end of the yarn with tape, making a "needle" for easier threading.

5. Thread the yarn through the holes, outlining the animal.

6. Using more yarn, connect the holes to "color in" the animal. Add another color yarn for its eyes, whiskers, etc.

2. Button Collage

You will need:
- A piece of fabric.
- Pencil or chalk.
- Needle.
- Scissors.
- Thread.
- Buttons of different types, colors, sizes, and shapes.

1. Place the fabric on a table.

2. Arrange the buttons on the fabric until you are happy with the design they make.

3. Carefully mark where each button belongs on the fabric. Remove the buttons and place them next to the fabric.

4. Sew on the buttons.

3. A Real Page Turner

Originally, books were sewn together using thread. You can use your sewing skills to make your own book.

You will need:
• 3 pieces of paper all the same size.
• Hole puncher.
• A piece of lightweight cardboard.
• Needle.
• Thick thread or yarn.
• Fabric or contact paper (optional).
• Tape or glue stick.

1. Fold the pieces of paper in half.

2. Fold the cardboard in half. Place the paper between the two halves of cardboard.

3. Thread the needle.

4. Punch holes through the paper and cardboard near the folded edge.

5. Carefully poke the needle through the back of the cardboard, then through the pages, two or three at a time. Once you've made it through all the pages and the front of the cardboard, turn your needle and stick it back through, just a little farther down the page. Keep doing this until you have stitched the entire book together.

6. If you want, cover the cardboard with contact paper or fabric, attaching it with glue or tape.

7. Use your book as a diary, a journal, or a sketchbook.

4. Embroidery

Embroidery is an art that uses thread to decorate fabrics. Each stitch gives the work a different look or texture. Try your hand at one of these:

You will need:
- Scrap of fabric (a different color from the thread).
- Embroidery thread.
- Embroidery needle.
- Embroidery hoop.

Place the fabric inside the embroidery hoop. This will stretch the fabric and make it easier to embroider. Use the pictures to guide you.

The stem stitch is used to outline designs.

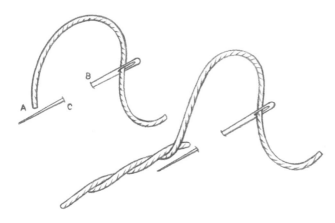

The satin stitch is used to fill in designs.

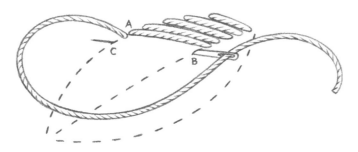

The cross-stitch is used to outline and fill in a design.

5. Sew What?

Use your sewing skills to make something useful. You can use this beanbag for lots of different games.

You will need:
- Two 4" x 4" pieces of fabric.
- Needle and thread.
- 1 cup of beans, sand, or flour.
- Scissors.
- Pins.

1. Pin the two pieces of fabric so that the outsides ("right sides") of the fabric are together—it should look like it's inside out.

2. Stitch the two pieces together on three sides. Make sure that your stitches are close together or the bag will leak.

3. Continue to stitch the fourth side, but stop when you've got one inch left unstitched.

4. Carefully turn the bag right side out. It may look a little squashed. Use your scissors to push out the corners of your squares.

5. Fill the bag with beans, or sand, or flour. Don't fill it too much, or you won't be able to stitch it closed!

6. Stitch the bag closed.

6. Patch It All Together

Make a patchwork quilt with your family or Girl Scout troop or group.

You will need:
• 4 squares of 4" x 4" fabric.
• Needle and thread.
• Pins.

1. Place the four pieces of fabric so they make one big square.

2. Turn them over so that the "wrong side," or back of the fabric, is showing.

3. Pin two of the squares of fabric together, with the front, or "right sides," together.

4. Stitch them together.

5. Repeat these steps with the other two squares.

6. Now pin and stitch the two bigger pieces together.

7. Turn the fabric over so the "right side" is showing.

This is how patchwork quilts are made. You can attach your four squares to the ones other girls make. Once everyone's four squares are put together, you'll have the front of the quilt.

To make the quilt usable, you'll have to put a backing on it. That means you need to sew it to a solid piece of fabric.

Try It!

Travel Right

Perhaps you're going to the park or beach with your family. Or you're planning an overnight at a friend's. Maybe your Girl Scout troop or group is going camping. It's going to be a lot of fun!

1. Be Prepared

List five "Safety Smart" rules to follow whenever you take a trip. Make individual checklists to put in your backpack or luggage.

Flash light
ex   clothes
food
drink
first aid
radio
toiletries
Book
Phone / wallet

2. Busy Kits

Put together a small bag of things to keep you busy on the road. Some items you might take are:

• Books (if you don't get carsick while reading).

• Song sheets so everyone can sing.

• "License plate bingo" cards and crayons.

• Cat's cradle string.

Make sure the bag is sturdy, and that your name is written on the outside. Use it with a friend the next time you're on a bus, train, or plane, or in a car.

3. Scenery Scavenger Hunt

Before you leave, make a list of 10 things that you expect to see on a trip. Check off the items as you go along. If you are traveling with a friend, you can each do a different list and see who gets all 10 first.

4. Travel Journal

Create a travel journal for your trip. Write a description of the places you went, the people you were with, and the things you did. What did you like the most about your trip? Why? Draw sketches of what you saw and did to go along with your written record. Collect souvenirs such as postcards, menus, and brochures.

5. Sing a Song

Make up a song about traveling. Sing it with your Girl Scout troop or group, or with your family on your next trip. Make up hand gestures to go with the song.

6. Pack It Up!

A day pack is great for almost any trip. If you are going on a hike, take along:

• A water bottle.

• A whistle—in case you get separated from your group.

• A rain poncho or windbreaker.

• Coins for the phone.

• Sunscreen and lip protection.

• A sit-upon.

Try It!

With a friend, list the things you would need to pack for these different trips:

An overnight at a friend's.

Sleeping Bag
pillow
tooth brush
Blanket
Pajamas

A 2-hour car ride.

food
drink
toys
games
pillow

A day at the beach.

Now, pack up the things on your list! Does it matter what goes in first? Where would you place something that is easily breakable? Is your pack more comfortable when you pack it one way rather than another? Is your pack too heavy? If so, is it possible you have packed too much?

81

Working It Out

Conflict happens when two people disagree. Learn how to handle conflict in a positive way.

wrong way

gime that

right way

can I play

1. Picture This

Draw two different cartoons. One should show the wrong way to handle a conflict—like hitting someone, having a temper tantrum, yelling at someone, or tattling. The other cartoon should show the right way to handle that same conflict.

Pick one of the following situations:

• Your brother or sister takes your toy.

• Someone at school is copying off your test paper.

• You disagree with your parent or guardian about how much time you're allowed to watch TV.

Share your drawings with a friend and see if she can guess which drawing shows the better way to handle these situations.

2. Clearing the Air

Sometimes conflict happens because what you heard someone say was **not** what she meant to say. Practice this listening activity to prevent misunderstandings.

1. Sit facing a friend.

2. Have her tell you something (it can be real or made up).

3. Start with "I heard you say…." and repeat exactly what you heard. End with "Is that what you meant?"

4. If she says no, ask her to rephrase what she said. Answer with "I heard you say…." and repeat exactly what you heard. Again end with "Is that what you meant?"

5. Continue the activity until the two of you agree about what was meant.

6. Switch roles.

3. Problem Solving

Sometimes it takes a person outside the situation to help solve a problem. With some friends, brainstorm a list of problems girls your age might have. Each girl should give an answer to one of the problems. Compare answers. You might find that there's more than one way to solve a problem.

4. Act It Out

Try this with your Girl Scout friends, family, or others.

1. Write out on separate slips of paper two problems you face, perhaps a bully in your life, a teacher who yells at you, or a friend who doesn't pay attention.

2. Place the two slips of paper containing the problems in a bowl.

3. Find a partner and pick out a problem from the bowl. Act out the problem together.

4. Everyone else watches and then offers solutions.

5. Act out one of the solutions that has been offered.

5. Negotiate

Negotiating is a way for people to come to an agreement. Negotiation can help solve lots of problems. In fact, some people make negotiating their full-time job!

1. With your family or Girl Scout troop, list three or four different situations that cause problems for you. Are you often late for school? Do you want a later bedtime? Does your sister take your things?

2. Go over one item on the list with a friend or grown-up and explain why it's a problem for you.

3. Brainstorm with someone why and when this problem happens.

4. Brainstorm a list of solutions to this problem. Pick one or two that might work for you and the other people who are involved.

5. Share your problem, your explanation, and your solution. Try that solution for a short time and see if things get better.

Try It!

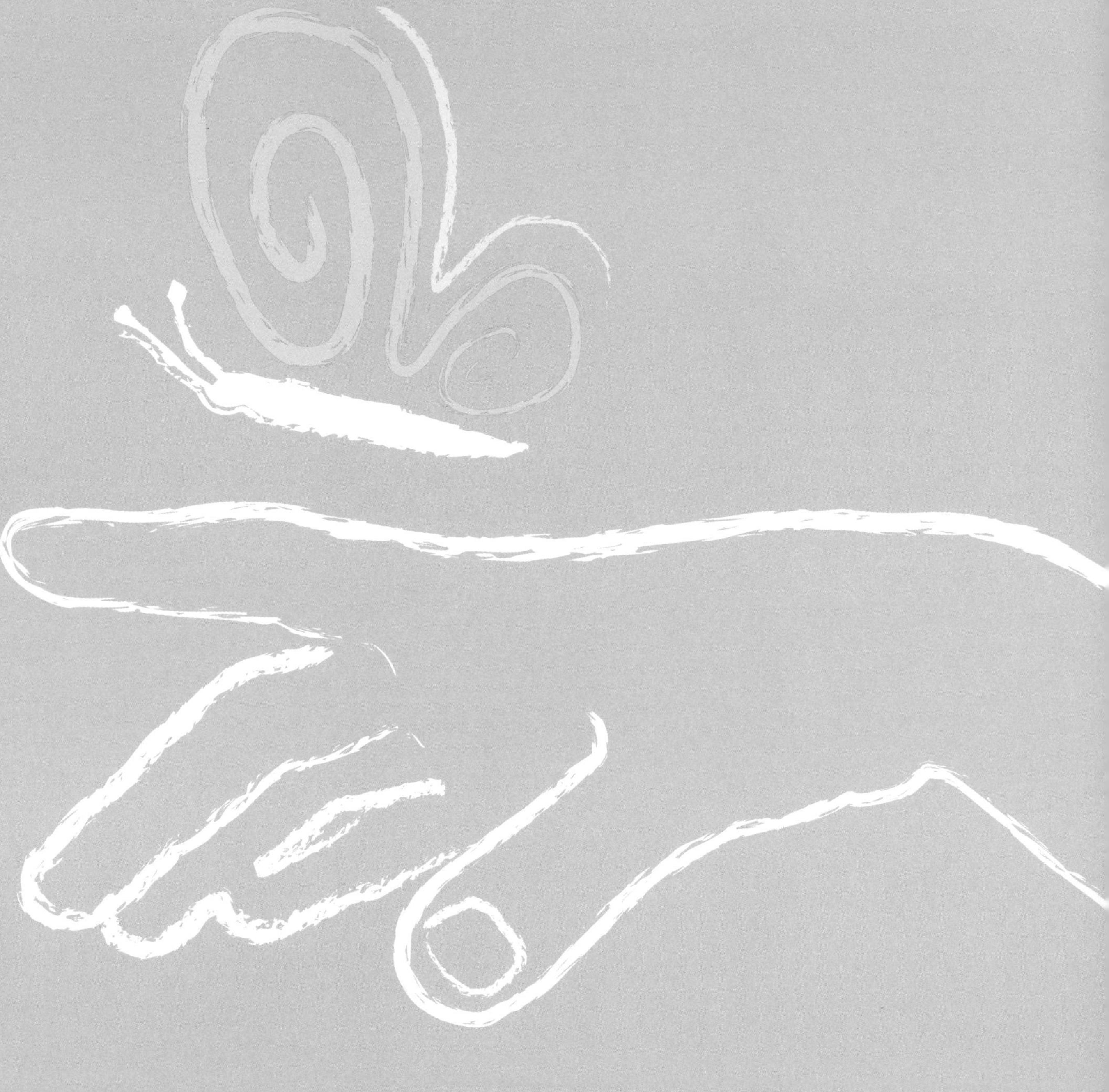

What's Out There?

Animals

Some animals, like cats and dogs, live with us as pets. Other animals, like moose and bears, live in the wild. Explore the world of animals in this Try-It.

1. Caring for Pets

Many people have pets at home—dogs, cats, rabbits, parakeets, hamsters, or guinea pigs. Do you have a pet? If you love your pet, there are special ways to treat it. See page 97 of the *Brownie Girl Scout Handbook* and take the pet pledge.

If you have a pet, help to take care of it for a few days. Along with a family member, feed it, brush it, walk it, give it fresh drinking water, or clean its litter box or cage. Don't forget to play with it gently, too!   OR

If you don't have a pet, pick an animal you would like to have. What does that animal need in order to stay healthy? Speak with someone who has that type of pet or go to a pet store that sells that type of animal and ask for other suggestions.

2. Understanding Animals

Visit a nature center, state park, or zoo. Find out how to enjoy wildlife in a safe way. Why is it best to watch wildlife from a distance? What are the differences between pets like dogs and cats and wild animals like squirrels and raccoons? Should you feed wild animals? What do you do if you find a baby bird that's fallen out of a nest or an animal that is hurt?

3. Creature Moves

Animals move in many different kinds of ways. Make the animal moves on page 87. You can play music that reminds you of how each kind of animal moves.

A. *Rabbit Hop:* Bend your knees and jump forward.

B. *Seal Slide:* Pull yourself forward with your hands at your side while dragging your body and feet. Bounce a little if you can.

C. *Elephant Walk:* Bend forward. Extend your arms and place one hand over the other to form a trunk. Make sure that your fingers are pointing toward the ground. Move slowly with legs stiff and straight and your trunk swinging from side to side.

D. *Crab Scuttle:* Sit on the floor with your hands behind you. Lift up your body with your hands and feet. Walk on all fours. Walk forward and backward quickly like this:

E. *Inchworm Crawl:* Place both hands on the floor. Try to keep your knees stiff and legs straight, but bend your knees if you have to. Walk forward with your hands as far as you can, and then walk forward with your feet to your hands.

F. *Frog Jump:* Squat on the floor with hands in front of feet. Jump forward and land on both hands and feet.

G. *Snake Slither:* Lie on the floor on your stomach. Keep your arms against the sides of your body. Move your body from side to side and try making an "S" shape.

4. Looks Mean Something

Animals are divided into groups by the kinds of bodies they have. Find animals that match the descriptions in the list that follows by observing them in a habitat (place where they live in nature), at the zoo, or in a book. How do their bodies affect the way they live?

- Animals that have 2 legs, 4 legs, 6 legs or 8 legs.
- Animals with no legs.
- Animals that have fur.
- Animals with feathers.
- Animals with scales.
- Animals that have shells.
- Animals with wings but no feathers.
- Animals with paws.
- Animals that have claws.
- Animals with flippers.
- Animals with hooves.

5. Sounds Charades

Animals communicate in many different ways. Some touch, some make noise, and some leave a smell. Play animal sounds charades. Have your friends guess which animal you are.

Here are some animals to include:

• Chicken	• Lion	• Parrot
• Fly	• Frog	• Alligator
• Cricket	• Elephant	• Monkey
• Horse	• Rattlesnake	• Cat
• Donkey	• Sea lion	• Mouse
• Sparrow	• Cow	• Owl

Write the name of each animal on a piece of paper. Put the pieces of paper in a bag and shake well. Pull out an animal name. Don't tell anyone. Show the others who you are by sounding like that animal.

Building Art

Architects, engineers, and decorators design buildings and other spaces. You can have fun learning about how museums, airports, railroad terminals, and other structures are designed and built and decorated by doing this Try-It!

1. Building for the Future

Choose a public building like a hospital, police station, library, or school. Make a model, poster, or sketch of what you think it might look like 100 years from now. Imagine what there will be instead of cars. How will people move about in the building?

2. Create a Neighborhood

Your neighborhood has special features—a park, garden, or playground, for example. Maybe the buildings have terraces or unusual windows. What's special about your neighborhood? What would you change to make it better?

Get a large piece of heavy paper or cardboard. Using pictures, small toys, clay models, and other materials, come up with a neighborhood that you would like to live in. Don't forget to include places like police and fire stations, a school, a hospital, and a library.

Compare your neighborhood with the ones created by other girls. How are they the same? How are they different? Did you forget to include anything important to the health and safety of the people who would live in your neighborhood?

3. Discovering the Strengths of Shapes

Making sure that a building will not crumble is an important part of what engineers and architects do. They experiment with materials and shapes to see how much weight they can hold. Use these steps to try it yourself.

You will need:
• Paper.
• A small stone or a coin or a button.

1. Hold a single sheet of paper by an edge so that it is straight over the floor. Place a small stone or coin or button on the paper. (See the picture.) What happens? The flat piece of paper does not have enough strength to hold the object.

2. Fold the paper in quarters like a book. Place the object on the paper. What happens? The paper has more strength because you have changed its shape.

3. Make a fan out of your paper. Balance the objects on the fan. What happens? The fan should support the objects.

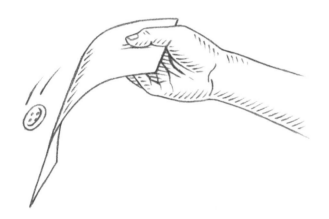

4. Experiment with other shapes. Can they hold up the stone, coin, or button?

4. Put on Your Hard Hat

Using only tape, paper, and scissors, make a model of a house, a store, or some other kind of building. Make a bridge, too. You might want to do this with your troop. Each girl can work on one building, or you can make the whole model together.

5. Designing an Ideal Girl Scout Meeting Place

Imagine the perfect meeting place that would allow you to do all of the things you'd like. Draw a picture or sketch or make a model that you can show to others.

6. Designing Space for Someone with Special Needs

What would you change about where you live or go to school to make them safer and easier to get around in for someone with a disability? You might make the doorways and halls wider for people who use wheelchairs. You could make a light flash when the telephone rings for people who do not hear too well. What else could you do?

Try It!

Colors and Shapes

Artists use colors, lines, and shapes to make art. Would you like to make art of your own? Develop your creativity with these activities.

1. Stencil Stampers

You can make your own stamps to use over and over. Use these designs to create your own greeting cards or wrapping paper.

You will need:
- Old sponges.
- Scissors.
- Poster or tempera paint.
- Pans to hold the paint (old pie tins or baking pans that you can throw away).
- Paper to paint on.
- Water (for cleanup).
- Construction paper.
- Paper.

1. Cut the sponges into the shapes you want.

2. Pour small amounts of paint into each pan.

3. Dip a sponge shape into one of the pans. Place it where you want on the paper and press. You can use this same shape over and over or you can add other shapes. Try other colors, too.

2. Colors and Shapes Mobile

A mobile is a work of art that can move. Try making your own mobile. Your mobile may tell a story or be on a subject that interests you. See the illustration for ideas.

You will need:
- 3 or 4 long plastic drinking straws.
- Fastener.
- Large needle.
- Thick thread or thin yarn cut into pieces of different lengths.
- Cardboard.
- Paints.
- Crayons or markers.

1. Thread the needle and tie a knot at the end of the thread. (Take care in using the needle. Be sure an adult is around to help.)

2. Use your needle to make a hole through the body of each straw and draw the thread through the hole. This attaches all the straws together.

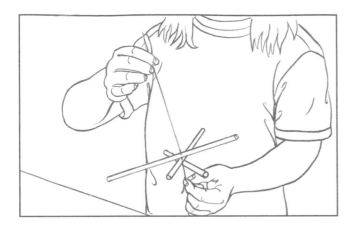

3. Cut the thread, but leave enough to hang the mobile.

4. Cut out shapes from the cardboard and make a small hole in each of them.

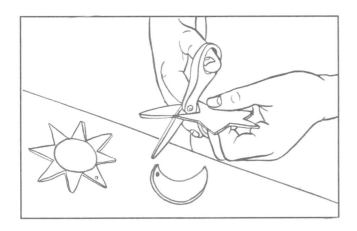

5. Using thread, attach each shape to the mobile. Move your shapes to different threads until your mobile has the right look.

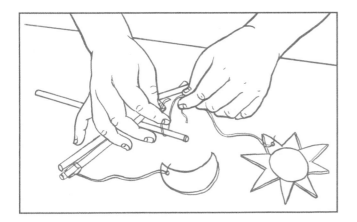

3. Making Dough Shapes

Would you like to mold and shape dough into all kinds of different objects? The first step is to learn how to make the dough itself, and it's easy to do.

You will need:
• 1 cup cornstarch.
• 1 cup salt.
• 1 1/2 cups flour.
• Water.
• A mixing bowl.
• A spoon.

1. Put 1 cup of cornstarch, 1 cup of salt, and 1 1/2 cups of flour in the bowl.

2. Stir.

3. Add 1/2 cup of water and stir.

4. If the dough is still too stiff and dry, add 1 or 2 spoonfuls of water and mix with your hands.

5. Make something with your dough. Here are some ideas: a bowl, an animal, a building, or a person.

Try It!

4. Weaving Color Patterns

You will need:
- Sheets of different-colored paper.
- Scissors.
- Ruler.
- Clear tape.
- A pencil.

1. Use the ruler to draw lines on the colored paper.

2. Make spaces between the lines the width of the ruler.

3. Cut the paper on the lines to make strips.

4. Lay eight or more strips of the same color next to each other evenly.

5. Tape them together very close to the top.

6. Take eight strips of another color.

7. One at a time, weave the strips in and out, as the picture shows.

8. If you started on the top for the first row of weaving, start at the bottom for the next one. See the picture.

9. After you have woven all the strips, cut the extra edges and tape them together.

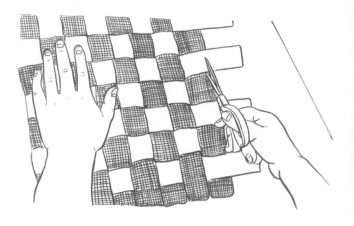

10. Turn your finished weaving over to see how it looks without the tape showing.

5. A Rainbow of Colors

You can learn how to mix your own colors while making your own painting. You can start with only three colors: red, blue, and yellow. These are called *primary* colors.

You will need:
- Poster paint or tempera in red, blue, and yellow.
- Paper cups.
- A paintbrush.
- Paper.
- A teaspoon.

1. Mix your three primary colors to form other colors. Follow this guide when you are ready to mix a color.

Red + blue = purple
Blue + yellow = green
Yellow + red = orange
Red + blue + yellow = brown

Use black and white paint to make more colors.

Red + white = pink
Blue + black = dark blue

2. Try some more combinations. What colors can you make?

3. Put 2 teaspoons of each of the colors you need in a cup and stir.

4. Now, you are ready to paint.

6. Yarn Painting

Yarn paintings are a beautiful way to combine colors and shapes. Many yarn paintings are of animals or flowers. Choose your own subject for your yarn painting. Maybe you will combine animals and flowers. Or maybe your yarn painting will be of a big tree that exists only in your imagination.

You will need:
• A piece of cardboard.
• A fine-tip pen.
• Different colors of yarn or string.
• Scissors.
• Glue.

1. Make an outline of your painting on the cardboard.

2. Cover the outline with white glue.

3. Press a piece of yarn into the glue on the outline.

4. Fill in small areas with glue and then the yarn, using your fingers and scissors to

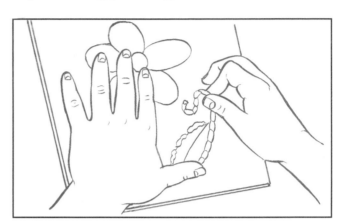

press the yarn pieces tightly together. Always work from the outside in winding your yarn so it fills in the spaces in the outline.

5. Let the glue dry and display your painting.

Earth and Sky

Look down. Look up. What do you see? Earth below and sky above!

1. Can You Dig It?

Find a spot with some loose soil in an outdoor area. You will need:

• A magnifying glass.
• A small trowel or garden spade.
• Tweezers.
• White paper or a plastic dish.
• 3' of string.

1. Make a circle on the ground with your string. Look on the surface inside the circle. What do you see? Are there any plants? What about animals? Is there anything else?

2. Use your trowel or spade to dig a hole about 1" deep in the ground. Make sure to stay inside your circle. Pick up some soil. What color is it? How does it feel? Are there any soil creatures? If so, use tweezers and gently put one or two in your white paper or plastic dish. Look at them with the magnifying glass. How would you describe these creatures to your friends?

3. Now dig a 3" hole and a 6" hole. How does the soil from these deeper holes feel? Is it the same color as the soil on the surface? Collect soil creatures from each hole. Put them on your white paper or in your plastic dish. Study them. Are they all the same? Do the animals living on the surface look the same as the ones living 6" below the ground?

4. Share your findings with your troop or group, or with a friend. Make sure to carefully fill in the holes again. Return the creatures to the soil. Leave your circle the way you found it.

2. Hot Time in the Sun

The sun gives heat and light. It dries wet fields and makes farm crops grow. The sun can do much good, but it can also do harm if we are not careful. For example, have you ever felt the pain of a sunburn?

• On a hot, sunny day, go outside and feel different objects in the sun and in the shade. Touch each one softly first to make sure you don't burn your hand. What objects were hot? Cold? Warm? Cool? If you have an outdoor thermometer, measure the temperature in the sun and in the shade. How much of a difference is there?

The heat from the sun turns water into water vapor—tiny drops of water in the air that you can't see. Heat makes water vapor rise in the air. This is called *evaporation*. Try the following experiment:

• Fill a dark cup or glass half-full of water. Stretch some plastic wrap tightly over the top. Put the cup where it is sunny and leave it alone. Look at it again in an hour. What happened?

3. Going, Going, Gone

On a walk or hike, search for places where soil has been worn down or has disappeared. Check the edges of streams or the sides of hills. What causes soil erosion?

To find out, build a big pile of soil about knee-high in your backyard or in a sandbox at a playground. This is your hill. Wet the hill with a watering can. What happens to your hill?

Now find a slope that is covered with grass or plants. Water it with your watering can. What happens? Is the result different from what happened to your own hill made of soil? If so, why? What do you think can be done to stop soil erosion?

Try It!

4. Sky Watching

The sky above can be fascinating. Be a sky watcher. Keep an eye on the clouds in the sky. How many different shapes do you see? What do the clouds look like on a rainy day? What do they look like on a sunny day?

Make a cloud picture.

You will need:
• Construction paper.
• Cotton balls.
• Glue.

1. Twist or cut the cotton balls into cloud shapes you saw in the sky.

2. Glue your clouds to the paper.

6. Make a Rock

When you're outside you can find many kinds of rocks. Some, like *sedimentary* rocks, are formed by mud and sand and other things.

Try this experiment to see how they form.

You will need:
- 1 teaspoon mixture of pebbles, sand, pieces of rock, and dirt.
- Plaster of Paris.
- Water.
- A paper cup.

1. Have an adult help you mix the plaster with water in the paper cup. Make 1/2 cup.

2. Stir the pebble mixture into the plaster in the cup.

3. After the plaster mix has dried, peel away the paper cup.

5. Creatures of the Air

Observe the creatures of the air. During the day, you might see different kinds of birds, butterflies, bees, and other insects. If you are lucky, just as it is turning dark, you might see bats. How do they fly? Watch as many of these creatures as you can. Take notes about what you see. Share what you discover.

7. What's an Eclipse?

There are two kinds of eclipses that happen in the sky. A solar eclipse is when the sun is all or partly hidden behind the moon. A lunar eclipse is when the moon is completely or partly darkened by the earth's shadow.

Here's a fun way to learn more about eclipses.

You will need:
• 2 balls of different sizes.
• A flashlight.
• 1 or 2 books.
• A table.
• A dark room.

The large ball will be the earth and the small ball will be the moon. The flashlight will be the sun.

Put the large ball on the table. Place the flashlight on the books and shine it at the large ball, or the earth. Hold the small ball, the moon, between the earth and the sun. Move the moon until you see its shadow touch the earth. Move it to the side so that its shadow moves across the earth. At one point, the moon causes a solar eclipse—the sun is hidden behind the moon.

Now place the small ball on the opposite side of the larger ball. Shine the light of the sun at the larger ball. Do you see how the moon is darkened by the earth's shadow? You have created an example of a lunar eclipse.

Try It!

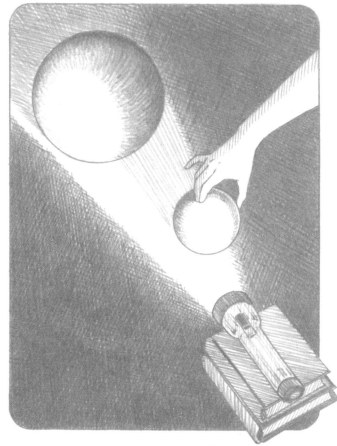

Earth Is Our Home

The earth is your home. Living things like people, plants, and animals make their home on our planet. How can you make your home a better place?

1. Clean and Green

Some of the chemicals in household products can harm people, animals, and plants. They pollute the air, water, and soil when they are sprayed, go down the drain, or are thrown away. How can you keep your home clean without harming the environment? Make natural cleaning products! Here are some you can try:

Glass Cleaner
- 1/2 cup of white vinegar.
- 1 quart (4 cups) of water.
- A spray bottle.

Mix the vinegar and the water in the spray bottle. Spray the glass with the mixture. Wipe off the dirt with a rag or newspaper.

Bathroom Cleanser
- Baking soda.
- Water.

Sprinkle baking soda on the sink, bathtub, or in the toilet bowl. Use a wet rag or toilet bowl brush to scour away dirt and stains. Warning: Don't use this cleanser on things that scratch easily.

Furniture Polish
- 1 ounce of lemon juice.
- 2 ounces of cooking oil.
- A plastic bottle.

Mix the lemon juice and the olive oil in a plastic bottle. Pour a little bit on the furniture and polish with a clean, soft cloth.

2. Project Recycle

Start a recycling center in your home or Girl Scout meeting place.

You will need:
- 4 big boxes or baskets. 1 will be for aluminum/metal, 1 for paper, 1 for plastic, and 1 for glass.
- A sign for each box or basket. Attach each sign to a box or basket.

Check with an adult to get a list of items that are recycled in your community. Here is a checklist to help you begin:

Aluminum
____ soda cans
____ aluminum foil
____ pie plates
____ frozen food trays

Other Metal
____ soup cans
____ dog or cat food cans
____ tuna fish cans

Plastic
____ milk containers
____ margarine tubs
____ water containers
____ vitamin bottles

Paper
____ newspaper
____ junk mail
____ magazines
____ grocery bags

Glass
____ tomato sauce jars
____ jelly or jam jars
____ juice bottles
____ oil or vinegar bottles

Can you find other items to add to these lists? Remember to clean and rinse out each container before placing it in the correct box or basket. Take the caps or rings off the cans, bottles, and jars. You can leave the paper labels on all the recyclable items.

3. Stop a Draft

Help seal up your house or meeting place. Keep cold air out and warm air inside by making draft stoppers. Draft stoppers help to close up the spaces and cracks under doors and along windowsills so energy is saved.

You will need:
- A few large pieces of cloth or old towels.
- Yarn or twine.
- Buttons, ribbons, lace, bells, etc.

Twist the cloth or towel into a tube-like shape. Tie it with the yarn or twine.

You can make your draft stopper look like an animal. Use buttons for the eyes or even for a nose. Or just decorate it.

Place your draft stopper against a crack in the bottom of the door or against a windowsill. You have become an energy saver.

4. Cooking with the Sun

You can use the sun's energy to cook your food in the outdoors. By doing this, you are saving wood or fuel. In some places in the United States, there is very little dead wood left on the forest floor.

Try making the solar bowl cooker below so you can toast some marshmallows the next time you go on a camping trip!

You will need:

• A large mixing bowl.
• A roll of aluminum foil.
• Marshmallows.
• Long, pointed stick or long fork.

1. Line the inside of the mixing bowl with aluminum foil. The foil should cover the inside of the bowl with the shiny side facing up.

2. Put your solar cooker in a bright, sunny place outside.

3. Now you must look for the hottest spot in your cooker. Place your hand over the bowl until you feel heat. This is where you should cook your marshmallow.

4. Put a marshmallow at the end of your long, pointed stick or fork. Happy toasting!

Try It!

5. Recipe for a Miniworld

A terrarium is a small, enclosed world made up of living things, soil, water, and air. Its covering lets in light.

The earth we live on is like a huge terrarium. Plants and animals need soil, water, air, and light in order to survive in both a terrarium and on the earth. If any of these things are missing or are damaged by pollution, the plants and animals will suffer.

Make your own terrarium.

You will need:

• A clear, wide-mouthed jar (like a peanut butter jar).
• 2 handfuls of small rocks or sand.
• 2 handfuls of soil.
• 1 handful of dead leaves.
• Some moss (look for it in a forest or vacant lot).
• Several small ferns or plants from a forest, a vacant lot, or a plant store. (**Do not pick protected plants or overpick an area. Ask permission to gather materials if you are not on your own property.**)

Follow these steps to make your terrarium:

1. Cover the bottom of the jar with the sand. Then cover the sand with the same amount of soil. Spread it out on top of the sand. Next, place the dead leaves on top of the soil.

2. Using a pencil, tongs, or a chopstick, make holes in the covering. Then plant your plants. Use the moss to fill in around the plants after you have tapped the soil down gently.

3. Water your miniworld with a squeeze bottle or sprinkle water with your hands. Do not put in too much water—the covering should not be soaked.

4. Place the lid on your jar. Keep the lid closed. Your miniworld should now have everything it needs. Place the jar in a place that has good light, but not in the direct sun.

Each day, watch for changes in your terrarium.

6. Earth's Caretakers

Adopt a special outdoor place in your community for two or three months. Pick a place where there are always people around. Make sure you have permission to work in the area you have chosen. Remember to wear work gloves and have the right tools for the job. Here are two ideas:

Help the Street Trees on Your Block
Loosen the soil in each tree pit (the square where the tree is planted). This will allow more water and air to get to the roots. Do this a few times during the spring, summer, or fall.

Plant Flowers
The spring is a great time to grow flowers in your neighborhood for everyone to enjoy. Plant them around street trees, at a school, or at a nursing home. Go back to water them and pull out any weeds every week or two weeks.

Eco-Explorer

"Eco" is short for *ecology.* Ecology is the study of how plants and animals live together in the environment. Have fun trying these activities as you become an eco-explorer.

1. Exploring Nature

Try to find both living and nonliving things in the natural environment. You'll need a pencil. When you find an item, check it off.

Do your best not to harm, move, or take away any of these things. Animals and plants may depend on them.

Nonliving Things

____ dew drops

____ smooth rock

____ shiny rock

____ sand

____ broken rock

____ water

____ sunlight

____ clouds

_ rock piles/cliffs

Living Things

____ flat green leaf

____ green leaf with pointy edges

____ green leaf with insect holes

____ green pine needles on a tree

____ insects (ant, caterpillar, beetle, butterfly, or any other)

____ flower

____ cactus

___ mushroom

___ moss

___ squirrel

___ chipmunk

___ bird

___ worm

Signs of Living Things

___ ant hill

___ bird nest

___ bones

___ broken twigs/branches

___ brown leaves lying on the ground

___ bits of fur/feathers

___ spider web

___ animal footprint

2. What's a Habitat?

Unscramble the words below. The clue underneath the blanks will help you. Then you will discover the four most important things that an animal (or plant) needs in order to survive.

1. ___ ___ ___ ___
   o f o d
   Clue: When you are hungry and your stomach is growling, you need to find some of this.

2. ___ ___ ___ ___ ___
   t a w r e
   Clue: When you are thirsty, this is the best liquid for you to drink, and it's not soda!

3. ___ ___ ___ ___ ___
   p a s e c
   Clue: This one word means a place to live and it rhymes with place.

4. ___ ___ ___ ___ ___ ___ ___
   t e l h s e r
   Clue: If you were outside and there was a bad storm, you would look for this type of place.

Check your answers on page 105.

Now you know what is found in a habitat. A habitat is the place where an animal (or plant) lives and finds the four things above that it needs to survive. It is like the animal's (or plant's) address.

3. Make a Habitat

Pick one of the animals from the following list (or any other one you like) and make a pretend habitat for it to live in. Don't forget to include food, water, and shelter for your animal!

- Squirrel.
- Lion.
- Shark.
- Bear.
- Hawk.
- Monkey.

Make a habitat in a shoebox with buttons, clay, colored construction paper, cotton balls, felt, tissue paper, pipe cleaners, and other materials.

Try It!

4. Food Chain

Plants make food for all living things and use the sun's energy to grow. When animals eat plants, they get energy. You also get energy from eating food. Your food may be plants or animals.

A food chain shows how energy is passed from one living thing to another. All food chains start with plants. You can make your own food chain.

You will need:
• 8 1/2" by 11" sheets of paper.
• Crayons or markers.
• Pencils.
• Tape.
• Pictures of plants and animals.

1. Cut a few pieces of paper in half the long way.

2. Find a picture of a plant or draw one. Tape it to one of these strips of paper.

3. Loop the ends of the strip of paper together and add tape to make a closed circle. You now have the first link in your food chain.

4. Find or draw a picture of something that can eat your plant. Tape it to another strip of paper. Put one end of the strip through the first link and tape the ends to make another closed circle. Now your food chain has two links.

5. Find or draw a picture of something that eats the animal that is eating your plant. Make a third loop. Follow the directions in Step 4.

6. Keep going.

Here are some food chain ideas for you to start with:

grass—prairie dog—rattlesnake
acorn—gray squirrel—red-tailed hawk
flower—beetle—skunk—great horned owl
mayfly—sunfish—wood stork—alligator

5. Speak Up for Animals!

Some animals that live on the earth are endangered. If we do not protect them, they will be gone forever.

Put together a show that will tell people more about endangered species.

1. Pick an animal from the list below or find another animal that lives near you that is endangered.

- Peregrine falcon.
- Black rhinoceros.
- Florida panther.
- Mountain gorilla.
- Galápagos tortoise.
- Karner blue butterfly.
- Black-footed ferret.
- Giant panda.
- Orangutan.

2. Look up why your animal is endangered. You can go to the library or ask an adult to help you search the Internet for information.

3. Write about why you feel it is important to save your animal, where your animal lives, and why it is endangered. What can people do to help?

4. You may want to choose some music for the opening and closing of your talk show. You can include animal sounds.

5. After you've put on your show once, you might like to invite your parents or another troop to come and see it!

6. Helping Wildlife

As a Girl Scout, you care about the earth. When you recite the Girl Scout Law, you promise to "use resources wisely." Pick at least one of the activities from the list that follows to help wild animals. Work with your leader or another adult.

You can:

- Put up bird nest boxes. You can find directions on how to make them in many bird books. You can even make them from old milk cartons. Or put out birdbaths. You can use big plastic saucers like the ones found under plant pots.
- Make brush piles by piling up lots of dead branches and leaves. Small animals, like snakes, toads, chipmunks, and turtles, often hide under them.
- Snip six-pack rings with a pair of scissors. You know, those plastic rings that are used to hold together six-packs of soda. Why? Because the rings can cause harm. Animals can get their necks or beaks caught in them. In many cases the animals can't eat, so they die.
- Plant a garden for butterflies. Butterflies are only attracted to certain flowers. Also, some flowers may not grow in your area. Check at the plant store to see which ones will be best for this project.
- Put out a bird feeder and keep it filled all winter.

Try It!

Answers to word scramble on page 103:
1. food 2. water 3. space 4. shelter

Her Story

An issue is a subject or topic that people may have strong feelings about and want to discuss. How can you learn about issues important to women and girls?

1. A Girl Scout's Story

Read about Juliette Gordon Low in your *Brownie Girl Scout Handbook*. Or check out her story online at www.girlscouts.org/girls. Then try to find a woman in your community who was a Girl Scout a long time ago. Invite her to speak to your troop, if possible, or interview her. Find out about her memories of being a Girl Scout.

2. Talk to Women

Ask five women to tell you about what they believe are the three most important issues facing women today. Make sure you ask women of different ages, from teenagers to women over 70 years old. Include at least two women from a race or ethnic group different from your own. How are the answers similar or different? Share what you learned with the other girls in your troop or group.

3. Create Tales

What are some of your favorite fables and fairy tales? Would these stories be different if they were written today? How would the girls and women in the story be different? Or would they be the same? Change a story to show how today's girls and women would think, feel, or act. Share your story with others. Write it down, draw a comic strip, or act it out.

4. A Ceremony to Honor Women

Plan a simple ceremony to honor women. You can recite poems written by girls or women. Or you might like to perform a skit or make up a song about a woman in history or in your community. If you can play an instrument, play along to the song. Invite women who are special to you to attend the ceremony.

5. Help in Your Community

Service is an important part of being a Girl Scout. Look at the section on service on page 92 of your handbook. Would you like to do a service project that helps women and children? Choose a service project you would like to do, with your leader's assistance, from the following list:

- Make baby bundles. Include supplies like diapers, baby wipes, and bottles. Donate them to a community agency.
- With your troop or group, make a quilt to give to a woman and her newborn baby at a local hospital.
- Collect toiletries like toothpaste, toothbrushes, deodorants, shampoo, combs, and hairbrushes and give them to a shelter that helps homeless women.

6. Your Story

Think about where you will be when you are a grown-up. Create a time line for yourself like the one below. Write in your time line what you would like to do or to have happen in your future.

Try It!

My time line

Age	
6	get a dog named Spotty
7	sell the most Girl Scout cookies
8	join the soccer league
9	learn to ride a horse
10	learn to play the tuba
11	make scenery for the school play
12	get a baby sitting job
13	run for class president
14	be goalie on the varsity soccer team
15	get a summer job
16	be a foreign exchange student
17	learn to drive a car
18	go to school to be a veterinarian
19	start a pet awareness group
20	help stray dogs and cats
21	vote in an election
22	travel to a distant land with Girl Scouts
23	play a solo in a concert
24	work in an animal clinic
25	have my own horse

Math Fun

Did you know that you use math every day? When you count money, or measure your height and weight, or tell time, you are using math.

1. My Numbers

Numbers are used to tell many things about you. How many toes do you have? How tall are you? How old are you? Make a "My Numbers" poster that tells all your important numbers facts.

2. Telling Time

Today, we have clocks with minute and hour hands and digital clocks (clocks that use numbers), too. People have been discovering ways to tell time for thousands of years. One invention was an hourglass. You can learn how to make your own hourglass.

You will need:
- Two 1-liter clear plastic bottles with caps.
- Sand or table salt.
- Package tape.
- A nail.
- A clock.

Follow this diagram to make your hourglass:
1. Fill one of the bottles with sand.

2. Use the nail to make a small hole in each bottle cap. Ask an adult to help.

3. Screw the caps on the bottle with sand and the empty bottle.

4. Place the empty bottle on top of the bottle with sand. The empty bottle should be upside down so the caps of both bottles are touching. Tape both bottles tightly so they are joined.

5. Turn the bottles over so the bottle with sand is on top. Look at your clock. How long does it take for all the sand to move from the top bottle to the bottom bottle? How can you change the amount of time that your hourglass tells? Think of some games you can play using your hourglass as a timer.

3. Can You Guess?

Find out how well your friends and family can guess amounts. Find a large jar with a lid. Fill it with seeds, beans, or marbles. Count each one as you fill the jar. Have at least five people guess the number of objects that are in the jar. Record their guesses and ask how they made them. Let them pick up the jar if they wish. Did anyone make a close guess?

Now it's your turn to guess amounts. Have a friend fill the jar with something different. Try to guess the amount.

5. Budget for Your Troop

When you or your troop plan an activity, you will usually need some money. Find out how much is in your troop fund. Then plan for two activities you would like to do. For example, the seven girls in Rosa's troop wanted to visit the zoo. They figured out what all the costs would be. Then they multiplied each cost (for example, entrance fee and lunch) by how many girls were going. To come up with the grand total for the troop, they added the amount of money needed for each activity in the column on the far right. See the sample planning chart below.

Zoo Cost	Cost for Each Girl		Number of Girls in Troop		Amount of Money Needed
Entrance fee	$4.00	x	7	=	$28.00
Lunch	$3.00	x	7	=	$21.00
Souvenir	$2.00	x	7	=	$14.00
Public Bus	$2.00	x	7	=	$14.00
			Grand Total:	=	$77.00

Do you have enough money in the troop fund?

4. Alphabet Code

Make up your own secret code. Write down the letters of the alphabet. Next to each letter put a different number from 1 to 26. You don't have to write the numbers in order. Use your code to send a secret message to a friend who knows the code.

6. Money Words

Give a dollar value to each letter of the alphabet. For example, A = 1¢, B = 2¢, C = 3¢, and so on. Then add up the cents that are in the letters of your first name.

What is the most expensive word or name you can think of? Find as many words as you can that add up to $1.00.

Movers

The wind can create a gentle breeze or make a powerful hurricane. An airplane couldn't fly without the wind blowing over its wings. Can the wind help you have fun? Do these activities to find out.

1. Pinwheel

Just like a windmill, a pinwheel uses wind energy to make it spin. Make your own pinwheel to see how this works.

You will need:
• A 6" square of construction paper.
• A ruler.
• Scissors.
• A straight pin.
• 2 beads.
• A pencil with an eraser.
• Masking tape or small piece of clay (if needed).

1. Using the ruler, draw a light pencil line from one corner to the opposite corner of the square of paper. Do the same with the other two corners.

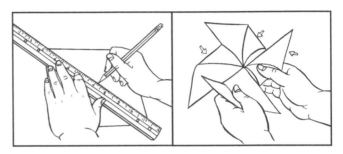

2. Make a cut 2" long along each of the lines from the corner toward the center.

3. Slide a bead onto the pin.

4. Fold the four blades as shown, but don't crease the folds!

5. Pass the pin through the center of the pinwheel. This will hold the four blades together.

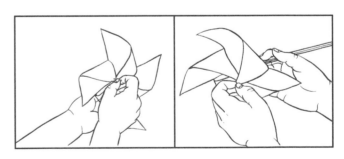

6. Slide the other bead onto the pin.

7. Stick the pin into the side of the eraser.

If the point of the pin comes through, cover it with tape or clay. You are now ready to give your pinwheel a whirl!

2. Paper Copter

Helicopters use whirling blades to move through the air. You can see how this works by making your own helicopter out of paper.

You will need:
- Helicopter pattern.
- A sheet of paper.
- A pencil.
- Scissors.
- A paper clip.

1. Trace the helicopter pattern onto a piece of paper.

2. Cut along the solid (not dotted) lines.

3. Fold the two helicopter blades in opposite directions along the dotted line.

4. Fold the sides of the helicopter toward the middle along the dotted lines.

5. Fold the bottom part of the helicopter up along the dotted lines.

6. Attach a paper clip to the very bottom of the helicopter.

7. Throw the helicopter into the air to see it whirl!

Can you make it turn faster or slower?

Try It!

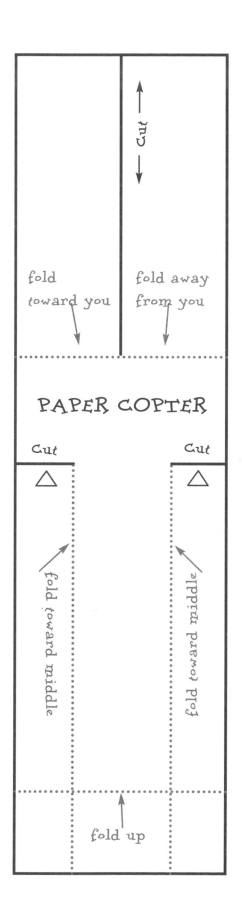

3. Ring Glider

Have you ever seen a glider with wings shaped like rings? These wings don't flap like a bird's, but they do help the glider move through the air. Try it!

You will need:
- A sheet of paper.
- Scissors.
- A plastic drinking straw.
- A ruler.
- Cellophane tape.

1. Cut one strip of paper that measures 7" long by 1" wide. Cut another strip that measures 5" long by 1/2" wide.

2. Make two rings out of the strips of paper by taping both ends as shown. Make sure the ends overlap by about 1".

3. Carefully slip one end of the straw in between the taped ends of the big ring. Do the same with the smaller ring. See the picture.

4. Check to make sure that the rings stand straight up from the straw. If they are crooked, the glider will not fly right. Tape the inside of each ring to the straw.

Here's how to make your glider fly: Hold the straw in the middle with the smaller ring in front, then throw it gently. You have liftoff!

4. Windsock

Make a windsock to find out the direction the wind is blowing.

You will need:
- A large sheet of construction paper (6" wide by 18" long).
- Crayons.
- Stickers (if you want).
- A ruler.
- Stapler.
- Tissue paper (about 2' long).
- A 30" piece of string.
- Glue.
- Masking tape.
- Scissors.

1. Decorate one side of the construction paper with crayons or stickers.

2. Make a ring by gluing the ends of the construction paper together. Make sure your design faces out!

3. Cut eight streamers 2' in length and paste them to the inside of the bottom of the ring.

4. Tape each end of the string to the inside of the top of the windsock to make a handle.

5. Hang the windsock outside where it won't get wet, then watch it play with the wind!

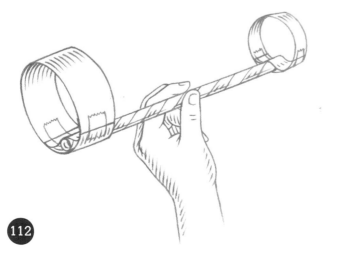

5. Lunch Bag Kite

Fill a lunch bag with wind to make a kite!

You will need:
- A paper lunch bag.
- Markers or crayons.
- Stickers (if you want).
- Scissors.
- Tape.
- A long piece of string.
- Tissue paper, ribbon, or lightweight fabric.
- Hole puncher.

1. Decorate the bag.

2. Tape 12" strips of tissue paper, ribbon, or fabric to the bottom of the bag.

3. Fold down 1" of the open end of the bag at the seam (where the bag is glued together).

4. Punch a hole through the folded-over part.

5. Put a piece of tape over the hole on the inside and outside of the bag.

6. Punch a hole in the tape with a pencil.

7. Tie one end of the string or yarn through the hole. Your kite is ready to fly!

6. Balloon Rocket

Rockets, like airplanes, need fuel to move through the air. When gases from this burning fuel are pushed out the back, the rocket shoots forward. You can make your own rocket to see how this works.

You will need:
- String about 10' long (nylon string works best).
- A long, thin balloon.
- Tape.
- A paper lunch bag (decorated).
- A drinking straw.

1. Slide the string through the straw.

2. Tie each end of the string to something (like two chairs). Pull the string tight. This is the track for your rocket.

3. Tape the paper bag to the straw as shown. Slide the paper bag to one end of the string.

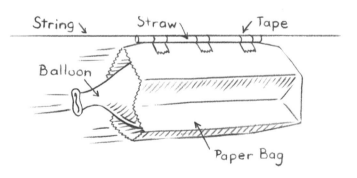

4. With an adult, blow up the balloon. This will be the "engine" of your rocket. Hold the balloon closed so that the air does not get out!

5. Launch your rocket by placing the balloon inside the bag, then letting go. Blast off!

Numbers and Shapes

Have some fun with numbers and shapes.

1. Math Shapes

Try to make different patterns from the same shapes.

You will need:
• Paper.
• Scissors.
• A ruler.
• A pencil.

1. Have someone help you trace or draw the different shapes inside the square shown here.

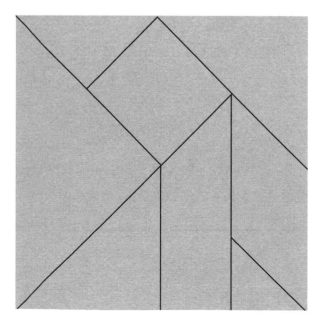

2. Cut the paper on the lines.

3. Try to remake the square by putting your shapes back together.

4. Try to make other patterns and designs.

2. Origami

Origami is the Japanese art of folding paper. Try making an origami cat.

You will need a square sheet of paper (you can make a paper rectangle into a square by copying these pictures).

1. Fold the square to make a triangle. See the picture.

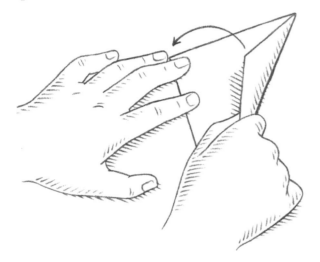

2. Fold the bottom part of the triangle up. This is called a trapezoid. See the picture.

3. Fold the right and left points up and to the front. See the picture.

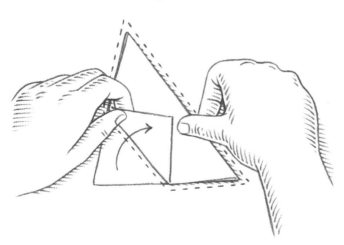

4. What do you have? You can draw a cat's face. What other animals or things can you make by folding paper?

Try It!

3. Möbius Strips

Simple paper magic can happen with Möbius strips. These paper strips are named after the German mathematician August F. Möbius.

You will need:
• Sheets of 8 1/2" by 11" paper.
• Scissors.
• Tape.
• A rule.
• A pencil.

1. Make a design on one side of the paper.

2. Draw long, straight lines 1" apart along the length of the paper. Use the ruler to help you space the lines and draw them straight.

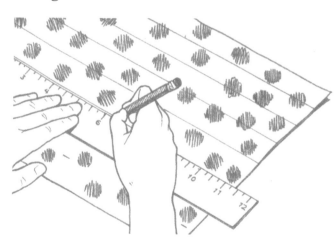

3. Cut the paper into strips along the lines.

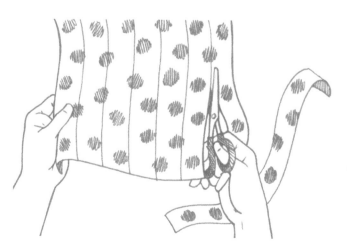

4. Make three different kinds of loops, as shown.

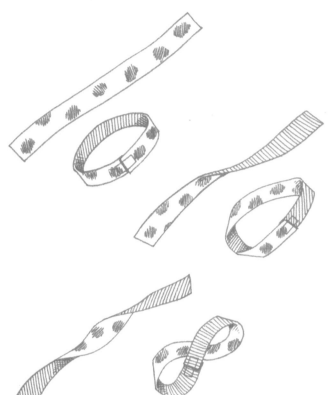

5. Tape the ends.

6. Without breaking the chains, cut the loops. Look at the picture to see how it's done.

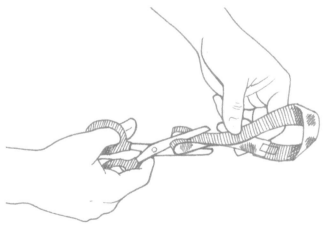

7. What happens? Feel your way around the edge of the Möbius strip.

4. Jigsaw Puzzles

Try to make your own puzzle.

You will need:
• Scissors.
• Heavy paper.
• Glue or paste.
• Newspaper or wax paper.
• Books or other heavy things.
• A pen.
• A picture of something you like.
• An envelope.

1. Spread a thin coat of glue on the heavy paper.

2. Put your picture on the gluey paper and press it smooth.

3. Dry the paper flat by covering it with newspaper or wax paper and laying books on top. Let the papers dry for one day or more.

4. Trim the edges of your paper.

5. Draw several lines over the back of your paper.

6. Cut the paper apart.

7. Try to put your puzzle back together.

8. Store the pieces of your puzzle in an envelope for safekeeping.

5. The Shapes of the Moon

Many people only think of the moon as a circle in the sky at night.

During one month, watch the moon to see how it changes its shape. Does it start out looking like a circle? Starting on the first day of the month, draw a picture of what the moon looks like once a week. On which day of the month does the moon look like a complete circle? On which day does it look like it is cut in half?

6. Nature Shapes

Take a walk in your neighborhood or a hike in a forest or park. Carry a pad and pencil with you. Look around and try to find different shapes in nature. Do you see any circles, squares, or triangles? Identify any natural things that are in the shape of ovals, diamonds, or straight lines. Draw something in nature that has at least one of these shapes in it.

Outdoor Adventurer

Outdoor activities are a special part of being a Brownie Girl Scout. So sleep out, hike out, eat out, and have some fun in the sun—or the rain!

1. Dress for the Weather Relay

Imagine you are walking through a field on a day hike and storm clouds quickly gather. You are wearing only shorts and a top when what you really need is rain gear.

Play this game with your troop or group before you go on an outdoor trip. It will be good practice for those times when you need to pack the right clothes for different kinds of weather.

You will need:
- 2 paper bags.
- 2 sets of clothes in adult size and for 2 different types of weather.

1. Divide into two teams.

2. Each team forms a line behind the starting point with a bag of clothes.

3. At a signal, one girl from each team puts on the clothes in the bag over what she is wearing. She moves as quickly as possible to a turnaround point. She returns to the starting line, takes the clothes off, and puts them in the bag. She then hands the bag to the next girl in line.

4. This continues until each girl has had a turn. The first team to finish sits down and the members raise their hands.

To make the game even more fun, place clothes for different kinds of weather in one bag. The team has to pick the right clothes for the kind of weather the group decides on.

2. Sleep Out!

Plan for and go on an overnight with your troop in someone's backyard or a council camp area.

Use this checklist:

___ Plan ahead. Discuss what you will do with the other girls in your troop.

___ Learn and practice the skills you will need to enjoy the outdoors. See pages 106–115 in the *Brownie Girl Scout Handbook*.

___ Dress right. Make sure your clothes are correct for the activities and the weather. Always be prepared! See the previous activity.

___ Keep safe. Learn the safety rules you need for the place where you will be sleeping out, and the safety rules for the equipment you will be using. See pages 62–69 in the *Brownie Girl Scout Handbook* for safety tips.

___ Leave the place better than you found it. Be prepared to take out your garbage and practice conservation in the outdoors.

Be sure to have some fun after dark, too. Sit around in a circle with your flashlights and tell some stories or share some jokes. Be careful never to shine your flashlight in someone else's eyes.

3. Day Hike

Plan a day hike in a forest, park, Girl Scout camp, or nature preserve.

Make a walking salad to take with you as your snack. You will need:
• Carrots.
• Celery sticks.
• Raisins.
• Apple slices dipped in lemon juice.

Do one of the following activities:

1. Follow a nature trail. If a map or guide is available, use it. Read the signs. They will often tell you the names of trees and plants. If you are quiet, you may even see some wildlife.

2. Try a color hike. Each girl decides on a color and looks for things that match that color.

3. Use a magnifying glass to find the smallest living things you can.

4. Build a Shelter

What would you do if you were hiking and got caught in a storm? With the other members of your troop or group, try to build a shelter. First, pick a spot. Then look for natural things around you that you could use to make a shelter. Maybe you have something in your day pack, like a rain poncho, that could become part of your shelter. You'll have to work together if you want to make a really good shelter!

After you've finished, talk about why you used the materials you did. Then take the shelter apart. Remember that you always should leave a place the way you found it— or better.

5. Touch, Smell, Listen

You can learn about the outside world by using all of your senses. In this hunt, you will need to use more than your eyes.

Find the things in the out-of-doors that match the descriptions on this list. After you discover something, touch and smell the object as a way of finding out more about it. But beware of poison ivy or other poisonous plants.

Smell

___ Something sweet-smelling
___ Something sour-smelling
___ Something flowcry
___ Something minty
___ Something bad-smelling
___ Something pinelike
___ Something lemony
___ Something fruity

Touch

___ Something rough
___ Something smooth
___ Something dull
___ Something pointy
___ Something soft
___ Something hard
___ Something bumpy
___ Something squishy
___ Something crumbly
___ Something wet

Listen

___ Leaves rustling
___ Twigs snapping
___ Birds singing
___ Birds flying
___ Animals moving
___ Water running
___ Insects buzzing
___ Wind moving things

Plants

Plants have many uses—food, lumber, medicine, paper—and they make oxygen that is part of the air you breathe.

1. Seed Race

Seeds take different amounts of time to grow. Try an experiment to see which seed wins a sprout race.

You will need:
- Potting soil.
- 6 kinds of seeds.
- 1/2 of an egg carton.
- A spoon.
- Water.

Fill each section of the egg carton with about two tablespoons of potting soil. Put one kind of seed in each section. Label each section. Cover the seeds with soil and sprinkle with water. Add some water every day.
Write down what you see happening each day. When did you see little green leaves pushing up through the dirt? How long did it take? Did some of these plants grow faster than others? Use a ruler to measure the height of each of the plants as they grow.

Move the plants to small pots with more soil. When they are bigger (at least 6" tall), try planting your sprouted seeds outside (if it's warm enough).

2. Plant Rubbings

A rubbing is one way to bring home something from the out-of-doors without harming nature.

You will need:
- Crayons.
- Plain white paper.
- Notebook with a hard cover or a table.

Lay your paper against the bark of a tree. Gently rub a crayon back and forth until a pattern starts to show. Pick up a leaf from the ground. Put it on a hard surface like a notebook with a hard cover or a table. Then place the paper over the leaf. Rub the crayon over the paper. You can make many different kinds of rubbings. Do any of the rubbing patterns look alike?

3. Baby Beans

Every seed has an *embryo* (baby plant) inside of it waiting to grow. The *seed coat* covers the seed and helps protect the embryo. The two halves of the seed provide food until the baby plant's real leaves can develop. Watch as a baby lima bean plant grows its first leaves, a stem, and roots.

You will need:
• 5 dry lima beans, soaked overnight.
• A wide-mouth jar.
• Paper towels.
• Water.

1. Fill the jar with wet paper towels.

2. Place the lima beans halfway down the jar between the paper towels and the side of the jar. Leave space between the seeds.

3. Place the jar in a bright spot, but not in direct sunlight.

4. Add water to the jar so that the paper towels stay moist all the time.

5. Watch what happens over the next week or two.

Did all of the seeds grow into plants? Which part of the plant grew first? How many days did it take for the plant to come out of the seed? Which part of each plant grows up? Which grows down? Why?

4. Leaf Hunt

Look for different types of leaves that have fallen to the ground. (Don't put your hands in your mouth after touching leaves and never put any leaves in your mouth. Be sure you wash your hands when you are done.) Pick one leaf that you like a lot. Describe it by drawing it or writing about it. You and your friends can put all your leaves in a pile. Describe your leaf to someone. Can she find it?

5. Simple Plants

Mold is a very simple plant that makes spores. Spores are like very small seeds. They are in the air and in dust. Try making some mold.

1. Wet a folded paper towel with water.

2. Wave some bread in the air and sprinkle it with dust.

3. Put the bread on the towel, wrap it in foil, and put it in a dark spot.

4. Check the bread every day. Rewrap it after checking. Use a toothpick to move the bread and wash your hands each time. Do not eat the moldy bread.

5. Draw a picture of what you see. A magnifying glass will help. What color(s) do you see? Does the bread smell?

Try It!

Ready, Set, Go Camping

What do you think of when you hear the word "camping"? You might think of sleeping in a tent or in a cabin. You might think of hiking in a forest or playing games. You might think of cooking over an outdoor fire. Camping can be a lot of fun when you're with other Girl Scouts and your leaders.

1. Roll-a-Bag Relay

Play the roll-a-bag relay so you can practice rolling up your sleeping bag or bedroll. You can also use two or more blankets tied together. (See "Making Knots" on page 109 in your handbook.)

Divide into two teams. Each team needs one sleeping bag. The first person runs with a sleeping bag to a line that has been set. She unrolls the bag and runs back to tag the second person. That person must run up to the bag, roll it up, and bring it back to the next person in line, and so on.

2. Bandanna Tricks

A bandanna is a wonderful thing to take on a camping trip. You can do many things with it. Fold a large bandanna so you can:

- Carry your lunch on a hike.
- Bring home the treasure you find on a trail.
- Wear it to keep your hair off your face.
- Wear it as a neckerchief.
- Use it as a cowboy mask on a dusty road.
- Make a hand puppet.
- Use it as a sit-upon.
- Use it as an apron.
- Use it as an emergency bandage.

Can you think of other ways to use a bandanna? In some countries, children carry their things to school in a bandanna. Japanese children call it a *furoshiki*.

Try It!

3. A Camp Stew for You

One-pot meals are easy to make and clean up after when you are on a camping trip. Work with an adult to prepare and cook a meal using this Girl Scout recipe for camp stew. You will need:

• 2 pounds hamburger.
• 1 onion, peeled and cut in small pieces.
• Two 10 3/4-ounce cans of condensed vegetable soup.
• 1/4 teaspoon of salt.
• Wooden spoon for stirring.

1. Add salt to the hamburger meat. Separate the meat into small pieces.

2. Put the meat in the bottom of the pot. Stir it as it heats.

3. When the hamburger is starting to brown, add the onion pieces. Stir the onion pieces until they are soft.

4. Add the vegetable soup and some water. Stir the mixture with a wooden spoon so it doesn't stick to the pot.

5. Cover the pot and cook the meat slowly until it is cooked all the way through. Serve the stew hot.

4. Storm Warning

There are many types of storms. Make up your own "group storm." In a clear space, each person acts out one part of a storm— the wind, thunder, lightning, clouds, rain, snow, hail, etc. Then create a giant storm by having everyone act out a part at the same time. How will each person's part change as the "weather" changes?

5. Knowing Your Knots

Practice tying a few simple knots before you go on a camping trip. This will help you wrap up your sleeping bag and other gear. Besides, it's a great skill to have!

An **overhand knot** is a knot on the end of a rope. This knot is made with one piece of rope. Follow the steps in the picture on page 21.

A **square knot** is used to tie two ropes together or to tie a package. It is also the knot used to tie a bandanna around your neck. Tie two pieces of rope together, following the steps on page 21. Remember this poem:

"Right over left and left over right
makes the knot neat and tidy and tight."

6. Hiking Scents

Go on a scent hike.

Ask a pair of girls or an adult to lay out a simple scent trail. They will need an onion or cotton swabs dipped in oil of clove or peppermint oil. Ask them to rub the scents on trees, rocks, or signs. Try to follow the trail by using your nose. What other types of strong-smelling things can be used to make a scent trail?

Create a scent trail for another group of Girl Scouts.

Science in Action

These activities will help you understand more about science in your life.

1. Science and Technology Hunt

Technology is a way of using science to create tools that make life easier for people. Go on a science and technology hunt! Each of the things on the following list is an example of science or technology at work. How many of them can you find?

- Something made of plastic.
- Something made from trees.
- Something that moves in a circle.
- Something that comes from the earth.
- Something that uses a switch.
- Something made of metal.
- Something that uses electricity.
- Something that uses wheels.
- Something that measures.
- Something that makes or uses sound.
- Something from the ocean.
- Something run by computers.

2. Weird Glop

Almost everything in the world is a solid, liquid, or gas. Things can change from solid to liquid to gas. Water can be a liquid or a solid or a gas. It changes to a solid when it freezes. When it boils and you see steam, it has become a gas.

Weird glop isn't really a solid or a liquid. Do not eat it!

In order to make glop, you will need:
- 1/2 cup cornstarch.
- 1/4 cup water.
- Spoon.
- Measuring cup.
- Bowl.
- Food coloring.

1. Pour the water into the bowl.

2. Add the cornstarch a little at a time while stirring.

3. Keep mixing until all your glop looks and feels the same.

How is weird glop different from water? How is it different from starch? Store the glop in a plastic bag. What can you do with it? Try adding food coloring to make blue, green, or red glop.

3. Balloon Blowing

Try to blow up a balloon without using your own breath. This will take several people working together.

You will need:
- 1/4 cup vinegar.
- A small plastic bottle (with a neck over which you can place the mouth of the balloon).
- 2 tablespoons of baking soda.
- A small balloon.

1. Pour the vinegar into the plastic bottle.

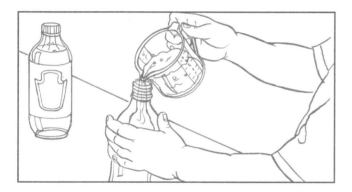

2. Stretch open the balloon mouth and carefully pour the baking soda into the balloon.

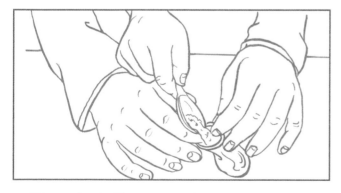

3. Place the balloon mouth over the bottle. Make sure that the balloon mouth is tightly around the neck of the soda bottle.

4. Hold the balloon to the side so that the baking soda does not fall into the bottle.

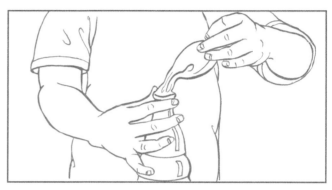

5. Shake the balloon so that the baking soda falls into the bottle.

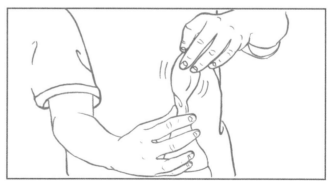

What happened? Can you figure out why?

Try It!

4. A Butterfly of Many Colors

The ink in a black felt-tip pen is made from chemicals of different colors. Mixed together, these colors look black. How can you see the different colors?

You will need:
• A black, water-soluble, felt-tip pen.
• A coffee filter.
• Scissors.
• 1 cup of water.

1. Fold your filter in half and cut out a butterfly shape, like this.

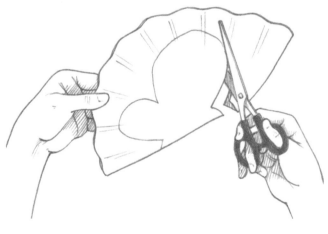

2. Using your felt-tip pen, run a heavy black line down the fold, like this.

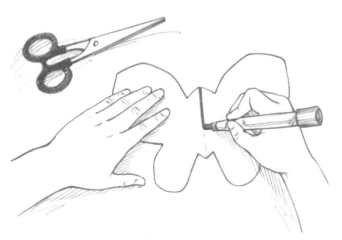

3. Dip the filter into the cup of water, like this.

Watch closely, but don't touch the filter. What happens?

5. Magnetic Box

Make a magnetic attraction box.

You will need:
• A small cardboard box (or plastic container with a top).
• Steel wool.
• Plastic wrap.
• A magnet.
• Tape.

1. Have an adult cut the steel wool into small pieces for you.

2. Place the pieces in the bottom of the box so that they cover the bottom completely.

3. Place a piece of plastic wrap over the top of the box. Tape the plastic wrap to the box.

4. Move the magnet underneath the steel wool pieces to make patterns on the bottom of the box.

What kind of patterns can you make? How far away can you hold the magnet and still make the steel wool move?

Try It!

6. Light and Color

All colors are made from three basic ones: red, yellow, and blue. These are called primary colors. How do you make other colors from these three colors?

You will need:
• Scissors.
• 4 flashlights.
• Red, blue, yellow, and green balloons.
• White wall or ceiling or white sheet of paper.
• Dark room.

1. Cut the necks off the balloons.

2. Stretch the balloons across the flashlights.

3. Turn off the lights in the room.

4. Shine the red light onto the white surface.

5. Shine the blue light onto the red.

What happens? What color do you get?

Red plus blue = _____

Red plus yellow = _____

Yellow plus blue = _____

Combine the green with red, yellow, or blue. What happens when you shine all four colors together?

Science Wonders

Try these activities to see how wonderful science is. The changes seem like magic, but a scientist can make them happen. And you get to be the scientist!

1. Home-Grown Crystals

Crystals are minerals that are clear and sparkly. Some crystals have colors, too! Ice, salt, and diamonds are all crystals. So is rock candy! Try growing some of your own crystals with this experiment.

You will need:
• Jar.
• Water brought to a boil.
• A saucepan.
• 1 cup of sugar.
• Clean string.
• Pencil.
• Paper clip.
• Plastic wrap.
• Magnifying glass (if you have one).

1. With the help of an adult, bring the water to a boil in the saucepan. Turn off the heat.

2. Add the sugar to the hot water a little at a time until no more sugar dissolves into the water. Stir a little bit each time you add the sugar.

3. When the sugar water cools a bit, pour it into the jar.

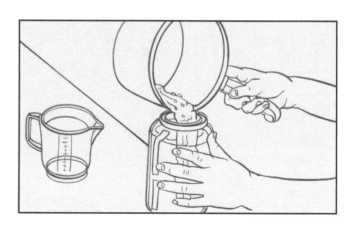

4. Tie one end of the string to the middle of the pencil. Attach the paper clip to the other end—this will keep the string hanging straight in the jar.

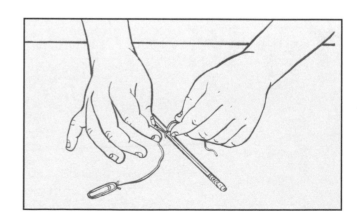

5. Wet the string with a little water, and then rub some sugar along the string.

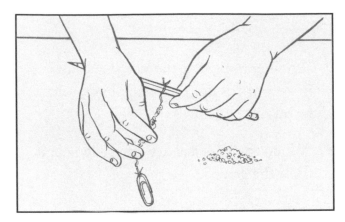

6. Place the pencil on the jar so that the string hangs down the middle of the jar. If the paper clip touches the bottom, make the string shorter.

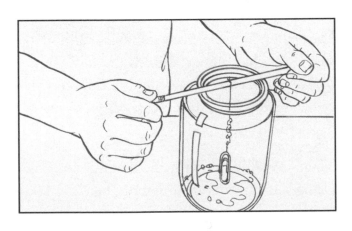

7. Place a piece of plastic wrap on top of the pencil and over the opening of the jar so that no dirt will fall into it.

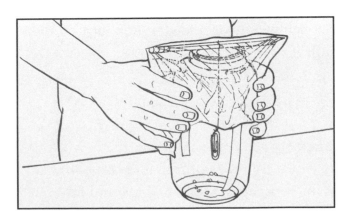

8. Put the jar in a place where no one will disturb it for a few days or weeks.

9. Take a close look at the sugar crystals that form on the string. Use a magnifying glass if you have one.

Do all of the crystals have the same shape? After you finish your observations, you can eat your crystals-on-a-string!

2. Bubbles

You can make some special bubbles. Try this mix:
- 1 gallon of water.
- 40 drops of glycerine.
- 1/2 cup dishwashing liquid.

Mix everything together in a large flat pan. Stir slowly. If you can, let it set for at least one day. The glycerine will make stronger bubbles if you do this.

For your bubble maker, have an adult help you shape a metal hanger. Dip your bubble maker into the pan and then gently wave it in the air. Try other shapes for your bubble makers.

Try It!

3. Homemade Recycled Paper

A fun way to recycle is by making your own paper. You can use this special paper to make note cards, books, collages, and many other things.

You will need:
- A large mixing bowl.
- An eggbeater.
- A cup.
- A big spoon.
- An old newspaper.
- Water.
- A screen about 3" square or bigger.
- A flat pan a little larger than the screen.
- Starch.

1. Tear a half-page of newspaper into very small pieces. Put the paper in a large mixing bowl full of water.

2. Let the paper soak for one hour.

3. Beat the paper with an eggbeater for 10 minutes. The paper should be soft and mushy. It is now called *pulp*.

4. Mix 2 tablespoons of starch in 1 cup of water. Add this to the pulp. Stir well. The starch makes the paper pulp strong.

5. Pour the pulp into the flat pan.

6. Slide the screen under the pulp. Carefully move the pan back and forth to form an even layer of pulp on top of the screen.

7. With two hands, lift the screen straight up (horizontally) out of the water. Place it on one half of the remaining newspaper.

8. Fold the other half of the newspaper over the screen and press down very hard. This will squeeze some of the water out of the pulp.

9. Carefully peel back the newspaper to uncover the pulp. Let the pulp dry overnight.

10. When the paper is dry, carefully peel it from the screen.

Try making paper out of other things, such as paper bags and gift wrap. Add lint from the clothes dryer, pieces of thread, tissue paper, or leaves for a special look.

4. Presto Change-O

Place about 5 tablespoons of skim milk in a small glass jar. Slowly add lemon juice (fresh or from concentrate) a drop at a time to the milk, stirring in between each drop. What happens?

Make invisible ink with the lemon juice. Using juice from a fresh lemon, take a toothpick and wet the tip in the lemon juice. Use the toothpick as a pen and the lemon juice as the ink. Let the paper dry. Warm the paper over a lamp bulb. What happens?

How is this different from what you saw happen when you added lemon juice to the milk?

5. Magnet Hunt

Magnets pull some things to them. Most magnets are made of iron and come in many different shapes. Get a magnet and find out what will stick to it.

1. Take your magnet and touch it to as many different things as you can find. See the chart below.

Magnet Hunt		
	Magnet Attracts	Magnet Does Not Attract
1. Straight pin		
2. Paper		
3. Aluminum foil		
4. Popsicle stick		
5. Penny		
6. Bean		
7. Paper clip		
8. Nut		
9.		
10.		
11.		

2. Check off on the chart all the things that are pulled to the magnet and all those that are not.

3. Touch the magnet to some other things. Add them to the blank spaces in your chart.

6. Static Electricity

A special kind of electricity, called *static electricity*, can be made by rubbing some things together. Lightning is a kind of static electricity in the clouds. The spark you sometimes feel when you touch something after walking on a rug is static electricity. You can try making your own *static electricity* with these activities.

You will need:
• Balloons.
• String.
• Very small pieces of paper.
• Wool cloth.

1. With an adult, blow up the balloons and tie the ends.

2. Rub a balloon very quickly on a wool cloth or your hair.

3. Hold the balloon over the very small pieces of paper. What happens?

4. Take two more balloons and tie a piece of string to each one.

5. Rub the balloons on the wool cloth.

6. Hold the balloons by the string and try to make them touch.

7. Rub another balloon on the wool cloth.

8. Hold the balloon next to a thin stream of water from a faucet. What happens?

9. Hold the same balloon to the wall. If it has enough static electricity, it will stick. Rub the balloon on the wool cloth again to give it more static charges.

Try It!

Senses

You learn about your world in many ways. Seeing, hearing, feeling, smelling, and tasting are the five senses that send messages to your brain about the world around you. You use your senses all the time, even when you don't know it!

1. Only the Nose Knows

Your sense of smell can be very helpful. For example, if food smells bad, you probably won't eat it. Here is a "smell" test to try out on a friend.

You will need:
• A paper or foam egg carton.
• A bandanna for a blindfold.
• Some paper and tape.
• Some "smelly" items.

You might start with the following: cinnamon powder, lemon peel, pepper, clove powder, nutmeg, chili powder, garlic powder, soap, toothpaste, or baby powder. Ask an adult to help you find more spices from the kitchen or other things with strong smells.

1. Break apart the egg carton into separate little cups.

2. Put a small amount of one thing to smell in each cup. Write on a piece of paper what each smell is and attach it to a cup.

3. Blindfold a friend. Have her guess what each smell is, using only her nose. Check her answers by reading the papers.

2. Making a Better Ear

Many animals depend upon their sense of hearing to find food. Do you ever wish that you could hear better? Let's see if you can make a better ear.

For this activity you are going to need:
• A loud ticking clock.
• Paper plates.
• Construction paper.
• Newspaper.
• Paper cups.

- Cardboard rolls from the middle of paper towels.
- Scissors.
- String.
- Glue.

With these materials, design a pair of ears that will hear the ticking of the clock before anyone else. Should they be small or should they be large? Should they be long or should they be short? Try it!

When you are ready to test your ears, have someone take the ticking clock across the room. Close your eyes and listen. You might want to turn your body so that your ears face the direction of the clock. The person with the clock will move closer to you. As soon as you hear the clock ticking, raise your hand and sit down. May the best ears win! Talk about what you have learned from this activity with the rest of the group. Can you find some pictures of animals that have ears like the ones that you made?

3. Now You See It

Can you always believe your eyes? Make a toy that uses your eyes to trick you. If you close your eyes tight, what do you see? You will see the last thing you were looking at.

You will need:
- A piece of heavy paper or light cardboard that is cut into a 2" square.
- Markers or crayons.
- A pencil.
- Some tape.

1. Hold the paper so that it looks like a diamond, not a square. On one side, in the middle of the paper, draw a fishbowl without the fish.

2. On the other side of the paper, draw a fish. Place your fish on the paper so that if you hold your paper up to the light, the fish would be swimming in the fishbowl. (See illustration.)

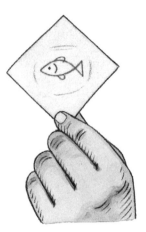

3. Tape your paper onto the pencil point, with the bottom of the diamond at the top of the pencil tip.

4. Hold the pencil upright between your hands. Rotate the pencil so the paper flips back and forth. Look at the paper. Where is the fish? Why do you think it is there?

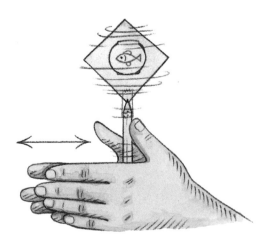

4. Can You Feel It?

Your sense of touch helps you find things in the dark and to tell hot from cold. Insects have antennae to help them feel their way around. You have hands.

For this activity you will need:
• 2 large paper bags.
• 2 of everything else (for example, sponges, dried beans, mittens, pennies, rubber bands, spoons). Make sure you do not pick anything sharp.

Put one of each thing into each of the paper bags. Shake the bags up, then reach into each bag without looking. Can you find the matching objects using only your sense of touch?

5. Mapping the Tongue

Think about different kinds of tastes. Mmmmmmm. They can be sweet, salty, sour, or bitter. When you eat something, does your whole tongue taste it? Find out how and where you taste things by making a map of your tongue.

You will need (for each person doing the activity):
• 4 small dishes or clean plastic film canisters.
• 1 teaspoon each of sugar, vinegar, and salt.
• 1 teaspoon of unsweetened grapefruit juice.
• 4 cotton-tipped swabs.
• A sheet of paper.
• 4 different-colored crayons or colored pencils.
• A cup of water for rinsing your mouth.

Do not share the dishes or the cotton swabs or the cup.

1. Place 1 teaspoon of each of the substances—sugar (sweet), vinegar (sour), salt (salty), and grapefruit juice (bitter)—into a different dish or canister. Add a little water to each of the first three.

2. Draw a big letter "U" on your paper. This is your tongue map.

3. Dip a cotton swab in the sweet solution. Touch it to at least four different parts of your tongue. Wherever you taste something sweet on your tongue, mark the same area on your tongue map in one color of crayon.

4. Rinse out your mouth very well with water. Use a different cotton swab and a different solution to do the next parts of your map for salty, bitter, and sour tastes. Rinse out your mouth between each solution.

5. You now have a map of your tongue's taste buds. Does your tongue taste the same flavors in the same spot? Where does your tongue taste things that are sweet, salty, sour, and bitter?

6. Compare your map with another girl's map. Are they the same?

6. What's It Like?

What is it like to be missing one of your senses? How do you communicate if you cannot hear? People who cannot hear often use sign language to communicate with others. Learn how to sign your name using the sign language alphabet on page 86 of the *Brownie Girl Scout Handbook* or learn how to say the Girl Scout Promise in American Sign Language.

Space Explorer

Learning about the stars and planets and other things up there in the sky can open up a whole new world. Astronomers and astronauts use telescopes, satellites, spaceships, and other scientific equipment to study space. You, too, can take a step into space exploration.

1. The Night Sky

Go stargazing with an adult who knows the planets and the stars, or have an adult help you read a star map. Try to find the North Star, the Big Dipper, the Little Dipper, or other groups of stars. (They are called *constellations*.)

Try It!

2. The Moon

Why does the moon look like it changes shape? One week it is full. The next time you see a half-moon. The moonlight you see is the sun shining on one side of the moon. As the earth and moon move around the sun, you see the moon in different places. You also see the parts of the moon that get sunlight. Draw the moon on the same day of the week for four weeks. What did you see?

Week 1	Week 2
Week 3	Week 4

3. Ready, Set, Jet!

Pretend that you are on a journey to a Girl Scout center on the moon. How would you dress for space? How would you move in space? Draw or create a costume for your journey. Show your drawing to others. Be ready to answer questions about your space outfit.

4. Shadow Time

Did you know that the earth rotates? It turns around much like a top. Have you seen the sun in different places in the sky? It looks like the sun is moving, but it is the earth that is moving. Try this activity to mark the earth's movement.

1. On a sunny day, take a stick and put it in the ground. It should cast a shadow. Mark the very end of the shadow by placing another stick in the ground.

2. Leave your sticks in the ground and return in an hour. Has something changed? Use a third stick to mark where your shadow is now. Do this once more in another hour. Which way did your shadow move? What do you think made your shadow move? Is there a way you could use this movement to tell time?

5. Star Maker

Pick a favorite constellation, or create a pattern of stars to make your own indoor star show!

You will need:
- A cylinder-shaped oatmeal container.
- A flashlight.
- A large safety pin.

1. Draw your constellation on the bottom of the cylinder-shaped container on the outside. Make dots to mark where the stars are in the constellation. Using the safety pins, punch holes in the box where you made the dots.

2. At night or in a darkened room, place the flashlight in the box and shine it on a blank wall or on the ceiling.

3. Show your constellation to others. Tell them about your constellation. Put on a star show with friends who have made their own constellation boxes.

Watching Wildlife

Have you ever taken a really close look at some of the animals that live in your neighborhood? If you do, you'll discover many interesting things about them.

1. Animal Architects

Many animals make homes or nests from paper, twigs, or wax. Find some animal homes in your neighborhood. Don't disturb these homes by touching them. Try to figure out what each is made of and which animal made it.

To find out what kinds of building materials the animals in your area like, try this:

1. Collect hair from a hairbrush, cotton balls, short pieces of string or yarn, and scraps of paper and cloth.

2. Place these items on a tray. Leave the tray outside on the ground. Or place the items in a mesh bag and hang the bag from a tree branch or other object.

3. Observe which animals collect the different building materials. (Spring is an especially good time to do this—do you know why?)

2. Animal Talk

You probably know what a dog means when it wags its tail or growls. A lot of animals use their bodies and their voices to communicate how they feel. Learn what some of the birds and other animals in your neighborhood mean when they chatter, flutter their wings, or shake their tails.

3. A New Wardrobe

Many animals change the color of their feathers or fur with the seasons. Pick some animals that you can see year-round in your community.

Birds, for example, are pretty easy to observe almost anywhere. Keep a watch on the animals you have chosen to see if they change color from one season to the next.

4. Earthworm Observations

How do earthworms move? How do they feel things? Can they see? Find out the answers to these questions by observing earthworms.

Here's what you'll need:
- Earthworms (from your backyard or a pet supply store).
- Paper towels.
- Water.
- Magnifying glass.
- Flashlight.

1. Wet the paper towel. Put an earthworm on the paper towel and observe how it moves. Earthworms breathe through their moist skin. If they dry up, they'll die—so keep the worm and paper towel moist!

2. Can you tell which end has the head?

3. Lightly touch the earthworm's back and belly. Do you feel a difference? Can you see a difference with the magnifying glass?

4. Shine the flashlight on the head end and the tail end of the earthworm. What happens? Do you think that earthworms can see light?

After you finish, make sure you put the earthworm where it will have soil to dig in. A park, backyard, or garden is a great place for earthworms.

5. Ant Adventure

Ants are very interesting animals. They live together in a group called a *colony*. All of the ants in a colony work to keep their nest healthy and safe. Some ants raise the young, some gather food, some defend the nest. Learn more about this very hard-working little insect by doing this activity.

You will need:
- Cookie, cracker, or bread crumbs.
- Magnifying glass, if you have one.

1. Look for ants in the cracks of a sidewalk, along the bases of buildings, or in a park.

2. Place some crumbs near an ant and see what it does.

3. Try using different kinds of crumbs to see if ants like one kind better than another. Does your ant tell other ants about the food it found? How can you tell?

6. Outdoor Shopping

When you need food, you go to a grocery store with a list. Wild animals need food, too, but they find the food they need in nature. Make believe that wild animals make a list of groceries when they search for food. Pick two of the animals in the list below and make a grocery list for each. Make sure to observe these animals for a few days before you make each list.

- Squirrel.
- Bird.
- Caterpillar.
- Deer.
- Raccoon.
- Butterfly.
- Fish.
- Dragonfly.
- Garter snake.
- Turtle.
- Ant.
- Spider.
- Rabbit.
- Earthworm.

Try It!

Water Everywhere

Find out about water without getting wet.

1. Made of Water

Water is part of more things than you may think. It's even part of you! Your body has more water in it than anything else.

Water mixes with other things so that it often doesn't look like water—milk and orange juice are two examples. Try to find food containers that list water as an ingredient. Make a list. Work with friends.

2. Drip Drop

A faucet leak that can fill up a cup in 10 minutes means that more than 3,000 gallons of water will be wasted in a year. That's about 50,000 glasses of water!

Find a faucet that leaks around your house, school, or camp. Put a measuring cup under it and time how long it takes to fill up. Add up how many cups of water are wasted in a day at this site. Try to get someone to fix the faucet.

3. Be a Water Saver

Make it a habit to conserve water. Practice two of the following for two weeks:

• Don't run the water when you are brushing your teeth. Start with 1/2 cup of water (you can add more if you need to).
• Take a short shower, no more than five minutes.
• Don't let the water run when washing the dishes. Instead, close the drain and fill the sink with water.
• Only fill up the tub halfway when taking a bath.

Think of one more way to save water. Practice that for two weeks, too.

4. Water Snooper

To build a water snooper, you will need:
• A large can.
• Clear plastic wrap.
• Rubber bands.

1. Have someone help you remove both ends of the large can.

2. Take the plastic wrap and put it on one end of the can.

3. Hold it in place with the rubber bands.

Use the water snooper to look into a pond or other body of water. Place the end with the plastic into the water. Make sure it doesn't just rest on the surface, but that it goes under the water.

Now, make a water-drop magnifying lens. Take a piece of clear plastic wrap and put two or three drops of water in the middle of it. Hold the plastic over the letters in this book. Are they larger? Hold the plastic over other objects. How do they look?

5. Water Explorer

Visit a pond, lake, small stream, or tidal pool at the seashore with your troop or group. Look for creatures and plants that live in the water.

You will need:
• A strainer.
• A white plastic bowl with water in it.

Dip the strainer in the pond or other body of water. You should not go into the water. Empty what you find into the white plastic bowl that has water in it. If you find living things, how do they move? What do the plants in the water look like?

Look under rocks in the water. Do creatures hide under them or cling to them?

Remember to leave the area as you found it.

6. Water Layers

You can see that salt water is different from fresh water in more ways than taste.

You will need:
• 2 glasses.
• Warm water.
• Container of salt.
• Food coloring.
• Spoon.
• Measuring cup.

1. Put 1 cup of water in a glass. Slowly add salt. Keep stirring. Stop when the salt won't dissolve and stays at the bottom.

2. Add some food coloring to the salty water.

3. Hold the spoon to the top of the water and very slowly pour 1 cup of fresh water onto the spoon. The fresh water will stay on top, because it is not as heavy as salt water.

Now do this experiment in reverse. Add salt water to fresh water. What happens? Next, try adding cold salty water to warm fresh water.

5

People Near and Far

Around the World

The world is made up of many different peoples and cultures. Try these activities to learn more about them.

1. Brownie Girl Scouts Around the World

Look at the chapter "People Near and Far" in the *Brownie Girl Scout Handbook*. What did you learn about Morocco, Finland, and Peru? Pick one of the activities in your handbook related to these countries and do it.

2. Look at the World

Here is a fun way to learn about the world.

1. Find the United States of America on a new map or globe. (The names of some countries change often.)

2. Look at the other countries on the map or globe. Name two countries close to the United States and two countries far away.

3. The equator is an imaginary line around the world that is an equal distance from the North Pole and the South Pole. The countries farthest from the equator have a very cold climate. Find the equator and follow it around the world on a map or globe.

4. Name 10 countries that you think would have a hot climate.

5. Name 10 countries that you think would have a cold climate.

3. Books

Many storybooks have been written about families from different countries. Visit a library and ask the librarian to help you find a story about a family from another country. Read the story, or have someone read it to you.

4. Global Family Card Game

Make a global family card game. Collect pictures of people from different countries. Make sure your pictures show people as they really live and dress. Don't use old pictures that may be out-of-date or inaccurate.

You will need:
- Magazines and newspapers (your library may give you magazines it no longer needs).
- Glue.
- Scissors.
- Index cards or light cardboard cut into 3" x 5" shapes.

Glue a picture onto one side of your card. Write the name of the country on the back of the card. Make up some games using your global family cards.

5. Troop Recipe Book

Some foods you like to eat may come from other countries. Have you ever had noodles, tortillas, egg rolls, peanut butter, or quiche? Where did they come from? Many foods also were first eaten here. Did you know that American Indians were the first to grow corn, which they called *maize*?

You can find out more information like this by making a "Troop Recipe Book." Bring in family recipes. Each girl can share information about her recipe. Where is it from? Who gave it to her? How do you make it? Put the recipes together in a book. Why not try them for a special lunch or supper?

6. Tapatan

In some countries, children play a game much like tic-tac-toe. In England it is called Noughts and Crosses. In Sweden it is Tripp Trapp Trull. And in the Philippines it is called Tapatan. Like tic-tac-toe, the object is always to get "three in a row."

Each player needs three moving pieces. They can be pebbles, buttons, or checkers.

1. Draw this diagram on paper or cardboard.

2. The game is played on the nine points where the lines meet. Players take turns putting their pieces on an empty point. This continues until all three pieces of each player are placed on the game board.

3. Player one moves one piece along a line to the next empty point. The pieces can be moved up or down or diagonally. Jumping over the pieces is not allowed. Player two does the same.

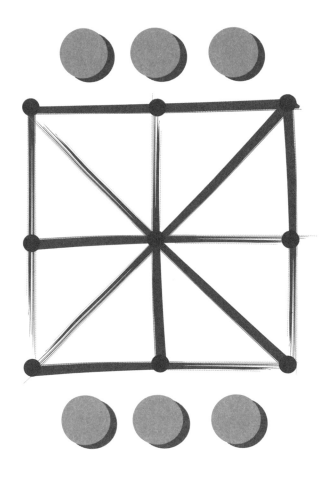

To win, a player must make a row of three across, up and down, or diagonally. If neither player can get three in a row, the game is called a draw.

Citizen Near and Far

You may be a citizen of the United States of America or of another country. You are also a citizen of the world. Good citizens obey the laws of their country. When you remember not to litter or when you recycle cans and newspapers, you are being a good citizen. You can do good deeds for your country and for the world.

1. Citizen of America

Learn about someone who acted like a good citizen. You can get the story from television, the radio, a newspaper, or a book. Share your story with your troop or group.

2. Getting Along

Think how boring life would be if everybody were the same. America has so many people from so many different countries, races, and religions. In a group, talk about situations that involve differences. Share an experience in which you or someone else was treated unfairly. Maybe you or someone you know was not allowed to be part of a group. How did you or the other person feel? What did you do? What else could you have done to fix the situation?

Discuss what you would do if these things happened:
- A friend said something bad about someone because of her religion or race.
- Some of your friends would not play with one of your friends because she speaks English with an accent.

3. It's the Law

Children as well as adults have laws to obey. Rules and laws help make things fair for all people. What special rules do you and the other Brownie Girl Scouts follow during your meetings? During trips you take? What might happen if you or your friends did not follow the rules? Share your ideas with your troop or group.

4. Making Choices and Voting

As citizens, you will help make the laws when you get older. You will do this by voting for laws and for people who make the laws. You may have already voted for something in your Brownie Girl Scout circle. What are some decisions your troop has made? What are some decisions your troop has to make?

It is important to listen to each choice before placing your vote. Practice making choices and voting. With the girls in your troop, decide on a fun activity for the next troop meeting. It could be playing a game or doing a project. Discuss each activity. Then take a vote. Talk about why the winning activity won the most votes.

5. Calling All Helpers

The United Nations is an organization that brings people together from many different countries and cultures of the world. The people talk about problems they share. They try to solve these problems.

1. As a troop, choose a problem that affects people all over the world. Here are some examples: pollution, violence, not being able to go to school, not getting medical care when you are sick, being hungry.

2. Ask your family and neighbors to suggest ways to solve the problem.

3. At your next troop meeting, hold a "United Nations" meeting. Each of you represents a part of the community. Take turns sharing with each other what members of the community had to say.

4. As a troop, think about everything that you heard. Then vote on the best way to handle the problem.

5. Share your solution with your family and neighbors.

6. Reaching Out

As a citizen of the world, you can help people in other countries with their problems. Find a group in your community that works to help people in other countries. Visit this group or ask someone from this group to come to your meeting to learn what she or he is doing to help people in other countries. Find out how you can help.

Try It!

Computer Smarts

The computer is not only a useful tool. It also opens a door to cool places, new ideas, and tons of information. "Be prepared" is a great motto for this Try-It. You should earn your Point, Click, and Go Try-It on pages 162-163 or have the skills needed for that Try-It before doing this one. To earn this Try-It, you must start with the first activity.

1. Be Prepared!

With an adult as your partner, learn to use an Internet browser. In the address slot, type in the address of the Girls Only Web site: www.gogirlsonly.org/internet_safety_pledge.asp. This tells your computer exactly where to go. Are you there yet? Next, read and discuss the Safety Pledge with your adult partner. Print it out and sign it.

2. Finding a Favorite

Travel to www.yahooligans.com, a search engine just for kids. Check out the categories with your adult partner and find one that interests you. Then use the search engine to find information about a topic. Share what you find with others.

Try It!

4. Surfing the Net

With your adult partner, find two sites for girls your age that end in the following:

".org"

1. www.gogirlsonly.org
2. _____

".com"

1. _____
2. _____

".gov"

1. _____
2. _____

5. Making a Chart

Learn how to make a chart with your computer. Make a kaper chart like the one below for a meeting, campout, or activity. If you have a color printer, experiment with coloring the letters and coloring cells in your table.

6. Computers and Work

Computers are needed in many different jobs. Talk with someone who uses a computer in her work. How does she use it? How does it make her job easier?

7. Computers at Play

Play an online game or puzzle that you find through Brownie Girl Scout "Links" on Girls Only at www.gogirlsonly.org.

BROWNIE	RESPONSIBILITY
Tanisha	tent
Kyoko	firewood
Megan	marshmallows
Rajani	juice
Nikki	bug spray
Kristen	cleanup
Rachel	flashlights
Zöe	marshmallow sticks
Amber	identification books
LEADER	RESPONSIBILITY
Mrs. Peterson	fire safety
Mrs. Han	tent setup
Mrs. Vidacovic	sandwiches

Creative Composing

Compose means "to put together," "to make up," "to create." Use your creative abilities by doing this Try-It.

1. Compose a Song

Make up a song for a special day or occasion: a rainy day song, a campfire song, a holiday song, a silly song, a song for a special Girl Scout ceremony. If you play an instrument, make up a song to sing with the instrument. Sing your song alone or with friends.

2. Compose Music for Instruments

Compose a tune for an instrument. It can be an instrument you have made. You can form a band with others and make music together.

3. Compose a Poem

Poems use words in special ways. Sometimes the words rhyme, which means they sound alike—out and shout, sing and ring.

Sometimes poems have lines that rhyme:

When I grow up,
I ll be a queen,
And never have
To eat a string bean.

Fill in the blanks in this rhyming poem.

I have a cat who

_____

It likes to play

_____

But not all poems do rhyme:

When I ride my bike,
I move so quickly,
I can t see the world.

Using images, write your own nonrhyming poem. Share your poems with your family or friends.

_____

_____

_____

4. Compose a Painting

Think of a special place. It can be a real place that you've seen or a make-believe place. Now draw it with a pencil on a piece of white paper.

In a painting, the things that are closest to you are usually drawn bigger. Things that are farther away are usually smaller. Look at where things are placed in your sketch. Should anything be moved? Made smaller? Made larger? Do you want to add anything to your sketch or change it in any way?

Next, think of colors. You can use watercolors, tempera, or poster paints. Hang your painting for others to see.

5. Compose a Play

Make up a play about something that happened to you one day—for example, in class, at home, on a picnic, on a playground, or during a vacation. Work with friends or create a one-person play. Perform your play for others to enjoy.

6. Compose a Message

There are many types of messages you can compose, and many ways to compose them. Choose one or more of these messages:

1. A secret message has a code that only you and the receiver of the message know. Before you write your message, you have to create a new alphabet. This is your code. The letter "A" might be a star, "B" a square, "C" a happy face, and so on.

2. Write a picture message. Cut out magazine pictures and use them to stand for words or phrases. Combine these with written words.

3. Compose a message using sign language and sign it to someone. Read about sign language on pages 86-87 of the *Brownie Girl Scout Handbook*.

Listening to the Past

When you listen to the past, what will you hear? You will hear stories about how people used to live and what children did a long time ago. When you listen to people talk about their past, you are participating in oral history. You can also listen to or see the past in museums, storybooks, skits, and movies. Listen carefully and see what you can learn.

1. Community Stories

Listen to the stories of some of the oldest people in your community. Find them through a senior citizens' organization, a religious group, a nursing home, or even in your family. Tape their stories or take notes. Share the stories with members of your family and your Brownie Girl Scout troop or group.

2. If These Buildings Could Talk

With an adult, visit the historic buildings, monuments, and sites in your neighborhood or in the nearest city. Learn an interesting story or fact about each.

3. Visit the Oldest Cemetery

Get permission to visit the oldest cemetery in your area. Do the following activities:

1. Find the oldest dates on the gravestones. Write them down. How old were the people when they died?

2. Write down some of the most unusual names. What is the most common name?

3. Take photographs, make rubbings, or draw pictures of the most unusual gravestones.

4. Tell Stories of the Past

Read two stories written in the past or about the past, and tell them to others.

5. Acting Out

Act out a scene from the past. Choose a favorite person or fictional character from the past. Do one of these activities:

1. Act out a scene from her life or from the fictional story.

2. Dress up like her and act like her during your Girl Scout meeting.

Here are some suggestions: Joan of Arc, Sacajawa, Anne Frank, Harriet Tubman, Helen Keller.

Try It!

6. Games of the Past

It may be hard to believe, but years ago your mother, father, grandparents, great-grandparents, aunts, and uncles were all young children. They played some fun games.

Here is a list:
• Dodge ball.
• Red light/green light.
• Tic-tac-toe.
• Simon says.
• Guess what I am.
• Kick the can.
• Jump rope rhymes.
• Jacks.
• Doggy, doggy, where is your bone?
• Crack the whip.
• Sharks and minnows.

Ask family members and neighbors if they have ever played any of these games. Then select a game and learn how to play it. Teach the game to others.

Making Music

Music is the art of making sounds. Different people find different sounds pleasing to the ear. Some sounds in nature, like birdcalls, are musical.

1. Move to the Music

Listen to different kinds of music—fast, slow, lots of instruments or voices, one instrument or one voice. Move your body to the beat of it. Twirl around. Jump up in the air. Take long leaps or make small, gentle movements. Make up movements set to music to tell a story.

2. Singing in Rounds

To sing in rounds, groups start singing a song at different times. Practice singing "Make New Friends" or "Row, Row, Row Your Boat." Your leader, another adult, or an older Girl Scout can teach these songs to you. Split into two groups. Group A sings first. When Group A reaches the second line of the song, Group B starts singing. What other songs can be sung in rounds?

3. Action Songs

Action songs connect words, music, and hand movements. "Bingo" is one and the "Brownie Smile Song" on page 15 of your handbook is another. Teach action songs that you know to a friend. Learn a new one from a friend.

4. Melody Glasses

Drinking glasses filled with different amounts of water can become a musical instrument.

You will need:
• 8 same-size drinking glasses.
• Water.
• Spoon.

1. Number the glasses from 1 through 8.

2. Fill each glass with the same amount of water shown in the picture.

3. Play "Twinkle, Twinkle, Little Star" on your melody glasses.

4. The numbers tell which glasses to tap. If a note doesn't sound just right, try adding or taking away a little water. Tap fast or slow in different places to follow the rhythm.

Twinkle, twinkle, little star, how I wonder what you are.
1   1   5   5   6 6   5   4   4   3 3   2   2   1

Up above the world so high, like a diamond in the sky.
5   5   4   4   3   2   1   5   5   4   4   3   2   1

Twinkle, twinkle, little star., how I wonder where you are.
1   1   5   5   6 6   5   4   4   3 3   2   2   1

5. Music Around the World

Sing the "Brownie Friend-Maker Song" set to a tune from Israel. Do you know other songs from different countries? Teach them to others.

Brownie Friend-Maker Song

KAY TEMPLETON   TRADITIONAL ISRAELI

2. Your Brownie hand in my Brownie
   hand,
   And my Brownie hand in your
   Brownie hand.
   We have Brownie friends in many
   lands,
   Across the seven seas, the mountains
   and the sands.

        Repeat chorus

3. Your Brownie hand in my Brownie
   hand.
   And my Brownie hand in your
   Brownie hand.
   On Thinking Day our love goes forth
   to ev'ry friend,
   A chain of Brownie hands reaching
   out, their help
   to lend.

        Repeat chorus

People of the World

You can learn many things from people who are different from you. Explore new worlds as you try these activities.

1. Language Hunt

Language is an important part of a person's background. Look through your handbook and other books. How many different languages can you find? Hint: Not all the languages are spoken. Name the languages that are spoken in your community.

2. Prejudice Fighter

In your *Brownie Girl Scout Handbook,* on page 128, read the "Fighting Prejudice" section of the chapter "People Near and Far." Then read the "Dr. M Letter" on the same page. Role-play the scene in the school lunchroom. Discuss it with your friends. Then decide on a different way the scene might end. Role-play that.

Try It!

3. World Stories

Close your eyes and put your finger on a globe or world map. Use your imagination to create a story about a girl your age who lives there. Share the story with your Girl Scout troop or group.

4. World Reporter

Interview someone who was born and lived for a few years in a country other than the U.S.A. Ask about things that are the same and things that are different in the two countries they've lived in. Ask how holidays are celebrated. Share what you've learned.

5. The Ocean Is Stormy— A Game from Denmark

This game uses the names of different fish. Do you know why this game is popular in Denmark? Find Denmark on a globe or map. You will see that it is near a lot of water.

Directions:

1. Use chalk or string to mark circles on the floor or ground.

2. Get into pairs. Each pair, except for one,

should stand in a circle and choose the name of a fish. The names of some fishes are: sea bass, trout, perch, catfish, herring, salmon pike, flounder, porgie, sunfish, sturgeon, bluefish, and blackfish.

3. The two girls who have not chosen fish names are the whales. They walk around the outside of the circles and call out names of fish.

4. When a pair's fish name is called, they leave the circle and walk behind the whales.

5. After all fish names are called, or after the whales call all the names they can think of, the whales shout, "The ocean is stormy!"

6. Then everybody rushes to find a circle. Any two girls can get in a circle.

The two girls left without a circle become the whales for the next game.

6. Flags of Many Countries

Every country has a flag. Each flag has certain colors and designs that make it different from the flags of other countries. People are proud of their flag because they love their country. In this country, you can see the American flag flying from public buildings like the post office, some banks and public schools, and even from private homes.

Look at the pictures of flags on this page. Select one of them. Learn what country it represents. Then find that country on the map. With crayons or paints, draw a picture of the flag and cut it out. Attach your flag to a stick with tape or glue. Plan a ceremony with other girls using the flags from different countries. Be sure to include a flag from the U.S.A.

Playing Around the World

Children all over the world play games. Here are some for you to try.

1. Kim's Game (England)

Girl Scouts and Girl Guides all over the world play this game. You and your friends can have fun playing it, too!

You will need:
- 1 or more friends.
- At least 10 small things.
- A scarf or piece of cloth.

1. Put 10 things on a table. Be sure you can cover all of them with the scarf or piece of cloth.

2. Show the players the 10 things for one minute. Then cover them.

3. Ask the players what was on the table. See if they can list all 10 things.

2. Red Light, Green Light (United States of America)

Here is one of many ways to play this game.

1. Choose someone to be "it." The person who is "it" stands at one end of the playing field, far away from all the other players.

2. The other players line up along the starting line at the opposite end of the field.

3. "It" turns her back to the group and yells "green light." The players may now run toward "it."

4. When "it" yells "red light," everyone must stop running and freeze. "It" turns around right after she yells "red light." If "it" catches anyone moving, that person has to go back to the starting line.

5. The game continues until someone has been able to reach and touch "it" while "it" has her back turned to the group.

6. That person becomes "it."

3. Sheep and Hyena (Sudan)

See if you can keep the sheep away from the hungry hyena! Get at least 10 people to play.

1. Players join hands and form a tight circle.

2. The hyena stays outside the circle. The sheep stays inside the circle.

3. The players in the circle have to try to keep the hyena from breaking through the circle to get to the sheep. The game ends when the hyena gets the sheep or gets too tired to go after the sheep anymore.

4. Two other people become the sheep and hyena.

4. Hawk and Hens (Zimbabwe)

This is a great chasing game for times when you have lots of energy and want to run. You will need at least four people and two safety zones.

1. One person is the hawk. All the other players are hens.

2. The hawk stands between the safety zones and tries to catch the hens as they run back and forth from one safety zone to the other.

3. When a hen is caught, she sits on the side and watches the game.

4. The last hen to be caught by the hawk becomes the next hawk.

5. Jan-Ken-Pon (Japan)

This is a game for two players.

1. Two players face each other with their hands behind them.

2. Together, they say "jan-ken-pon." On "pon," both bring a hand forward to stand for a stone (a fist), paper (flat hand), or scissors (V-shape with the index finger and middle finger).

3. Stone beats scissors because it can break them. Scissors beat paper because they can cut it. Paper beats stone because paper can wrap up the stone.

4. A player gets a point each time her hand beats the other's. The first player who gets seven points wins.

Point, Click, and Go

Learning how to use a computer is fun. The computer can help bring your ideas to life with words, pictures, colors, and numbers. You need to take care of your computer by keeping it safe from food and spills. Magnets can also hurt computers and disks, so they should not be kept nearby.

1. Making the Computer Work

If you have not used a computer before, ask someone to teach you:

- How to turn on the computer and start a program you want to use.
- How to use a mouse to make the computer do the jobs you want it to do. Point, click, go!
- How to handle disks and CD-ROMs to keep them clean.
- How and where to save something you create.
- How to print your work.
- How to turn off the computer when you are finished.

2. Computer Language

Learn the meanings of some special computer words and you will have an easier time communicating in our world of technology.

- Software
- Program
- Database
- Hardware
- Icon
- Font
- Memory
- Laptop computer
- Desktop computer
- Your computer's desktop

As you hear other new computer words, do some detective work to learn their meanings, too.

3. Writing a Story

Use a computer to write your own story or poem or write a group story with your friends. One girl writes the first sentence. Someone else writes the next sentence. And so on.

Your computer may be able to check your spelling. If so, does your story have spelling errors? Correct any errors and print your story. Add colorful drawings.

Mom called from the den.

"Here Kitty, here Kitty," said Mom. Susie, my callico cat didn't come. <u>Red paw prints were all over</u>   <u>the carpet</u>

4. Playing a Game

Lots of games have been made for computers. With the help of someone in your family or a teacher, get a computer game and play it. What do you like about the game? How would you change it to make it more fun? Harder? Easier?

5. Creating

Use a computer to make an invitation to a party, write a thank-you note, or make your own stationery. Print your creation and share it with others.

6. Talk Time

Some computers are linked together by telephone lines so that people can send messages to each other. Ask an adult to go "online" with you and send messages to other girls who are using computers. Many computer online services provide safe places for kids to talk to each other. They are called "chat rooms." Talk to a parent or guardian or a teacher about a time when you can talk with other girls together.

Try It!

Sounds of Music

What makes music different from noise? Music is different from noise because it usually has a regular sound or rhythm. If you think about it, some noises, such as the drip, drip, drip of a faucet, can sound like music. What other noises inside or outside can sound like music? Create some instruments to make your own music?

1. Make Your Own

Percussion instruments make a sound when hit or shaken. They can be drums, rattles, gongs, tambourines, or shakers. Try making a shaker.

You will need:
• A paper plate.
• Dry beans, rice, sand, or other small things that rattle.
• A stapler with staples.

Place the beans on the paper plate and fold it in half. Then staple the plate halves together so the beans will not fall out. Make one shaker for each hand.

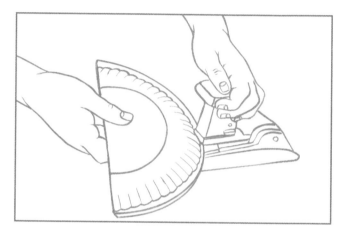

2. Single String Swing

Can one string make music? Try your hand at this one:

You will need:
• A large clean empty can (#10 size or 48 ounces) that is open at one end.
• A nail.
• A hammer.
• A heavy string.
• A pencil.

1. Ask an adult to help you use the hammer and nail to punch a hole in the middle of the can bottom.

2. Cut a length of string that goes from the floor to the middle of your thigh.

3. Knot the end of your string. Pull the other end through the inside of the can and through the hole you made. Make sure the knot is big enough so that it keeps the string from pulling all the way through.

4. Tie the other end of the string around the middle of a pencil.

5. To play your instrument, place one foot on the floor and the other foot on top of the can. Pull the string straight up from the floor so that it is stretched tight with one hand. Now, pluck the string with the forefinger of the other hand. Experiment with your fiddle sound by plucking in different places on the string. Try holding the string tighter or looser. How does the sound change? Can you get different sounds by changing the length of the string?

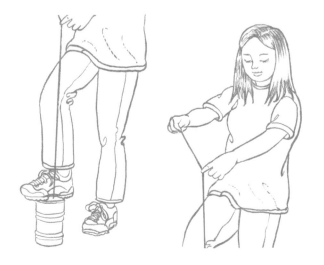

3. Sliding Air

What does wind have to do with music? Different sounds are made by changing the amount of air in a tube. Try making this wind instrument.

You will need:
- A straw.
- Water.
- A plastic soda bottle.

1. Fill the soda bottle about three-fourths full with water. See the picture.

2. Place the straw in the water and blow across the tip of the straw.

3. Lift the straw and lower it, continuing to blow. What happens? What is happening to the air in the straw as you slide it up in the water and as you slide it down? How does that affect the sound? When is the sound the highest? When is it lowest?

4. Shoebox Guitar

Did you ever think that you could make music with some rubber bands, a shoe box, and a paper towel roll? Here's one way.

You will need:

- A shoebox.
- 5 rubber bands.
- A paper towel roll.
- Tape.

1. Tape the cover to the shoebox and turn the box upside down.

2. Cut a large oval hole in the bottom of the box.

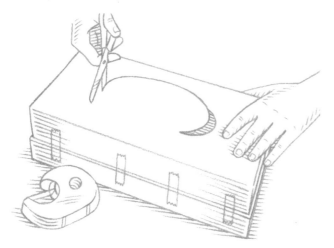

3. Cut a round hole on one side of the shoebox, just large enough to fit the paper towel roll through it. (Do not slide it too far in. It should not show through the front oval hole covered by the rubber bands.)

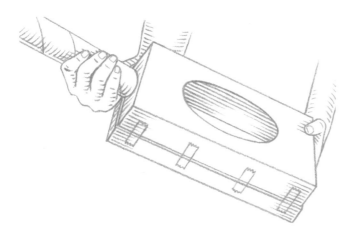

4. Tape the towel roll through the hole.

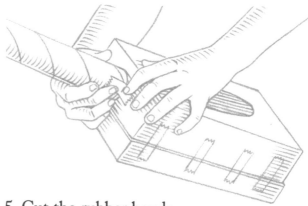

5. Cut the rubber bands.

6. Stretch each rubber band tightly over the hole in the shoebox, and tape each one down. (Leave a little space between each rubber band.)

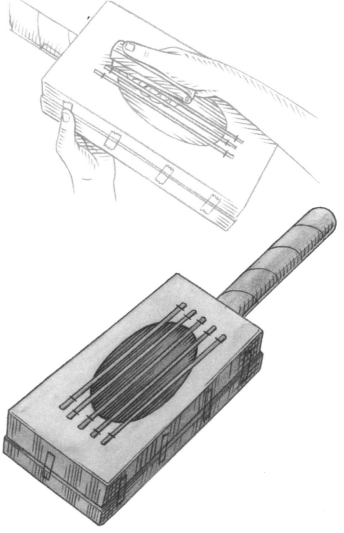

5. Melody Mobiles

Create a mobile that makes music as it sways in the air. First collect small, lightweight items that sound pleasant to you when they bump into each other. Check this out by dangling the items from a string and making them knock into each other. They can be pieces of hardware such as screws, small toys, old pieces of jewelry, hair clips, and other found treasures around the house. Select between 8 and 12 items.

You will need:
- 2 wire hangers.
- 2 pipe cleaners.
- Heavy string or yarn.
- The items you've selected.

1. Twist one pipe cleaner around the two hooks so that the hangers are joined at the top.

2. Twist the other pipe cleaner around the center of the bottom of the hangers, so that they are also joined together there with about 2" between the hangers.

3. Cut 8 to 12 pieces of string at different lengths: 4 pieces can be 14" long, 4 pieces 12" long, and 4 pieces 10" long.

4. Tie the strings to the bottom of the mobile hanger. You should have the same number on each hanger so the mobile will not be crooked.

5. Tie your items to the end of each string.

6. Hang your mobile and listen to the sounds it makes.

6. Live Music

Attend a concert put on by a band or orchestra. Are any of the instruments like the ones you made?

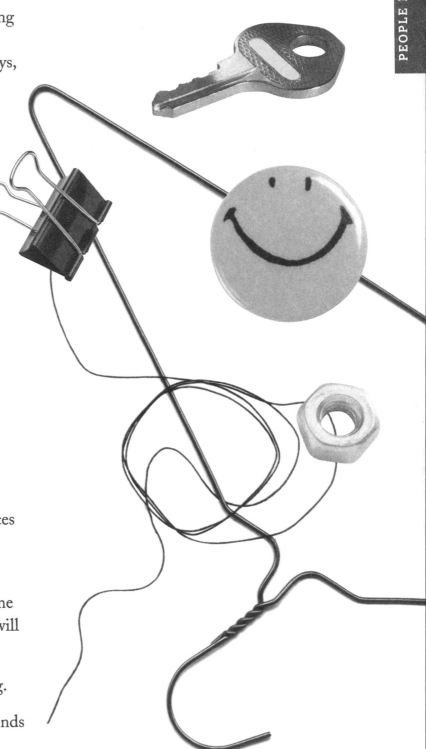

167

Index